ACCIDENTS IN NORTH AMERICAN MOUNTAINEERING

VOLUME 10 • NUMBER 1 • ISSUE 64
2011

THE AMERICAN ALPINE CLUB
GOLDEN, CO

THE ALPINE CLUB OF CANADA
BANFF, ALBERTA

ISSN: 0065-082X
ISBN: 978-1-933056-73-9
ISBN: (e-books) 978-1-933056-74-6

Manufactured in the United States

Published by:
The American Alpine Club
710 Tenth Street, Suite 100
Golden, CO 80401
www.americanalpineclub.org

Cover Illustrations
Front: Mark Vermeal enjoying one clean line. The route is called "Cocaine" and is located at Frankenstein Cliffs, NH. Photograph by Peter Doucette, who can be found at mountainsenseguides.com

Back: Lightning-fried ice ax (photograph by Jeff Witt, Exum Guide) and rack (photograph by Angus M. Thuermer, Jr., reporter for the *Jackson Hole News and Guide*). This evidence comes from the intense storm on the Grand Teton on July 21 that included lightning that struck 17 climbers. See the full story under Wyoming in this issue of ANAM.

Printed on recycled paper

CONTENTS

SAFETY ADVISORY COUNCIL 2010

ACCIDENTS IN
NORTH AMERICAN MOUNTAINEERING
Sixty-fourth Annual Report of The American Alpine Club

This is the sixty-fourth issue of Accidents in North American Mountain-eering.

Canada: Data and narratives not available from 2010. Visit alpineclubof-canada.ca/services/safety/index.html for information on the Alpine Club of Canada's safety program.

United States: Aside from once again seeing too many belay and rappel errors, it was a year with some major events. Among them: Another runaway sled incident on the Kahiltna Glacier—resulting in a fatality; an avalanche in the Ruth Gorge that resulted in the death of two experienced climbers; a HACE fatality on Mount Shasta; a rappel rigging error by an experienced climber on Serenity Crack in Yosemite (see illustration with this narra-tive); the aggressive and tenacious French climber on the Salathé Wall of El Capitan who did not give up on his grievously injured partner; the lead climber in American Fork Canyon, UT, who was pulled off by his belayer due to, among other matters, mis-communication; the eleven climbers who ignored the avalanche conditions on the Ingraham Direct, Mount Rainier, and were partly buried as a result; and the 17 climbers struck by lightning on the Grand Teton in August.

As mentioned in previous issues and throughout this report, there are some Web-based resources that often provide good information and ac-cident stories. Here is a short-list of some of those sites:

home.nps.gov/applications/morningreport
supertopo.com
mountainproject.com
tuckerman.org
mountrainierclimbing.blogspot.com
friendsofyosar.org

A few words about three individuals who are helping with important aspects of ANAM.

Molly Allen has been responsible for the layout of this publication for over fifteen years now. Though she is not responsible for mechanical errors or typos, she has a keen eye for these matters and often saves us a lot of time by making corrections as she goes.

Aram Attarian has taken on gathering reports from Colorado and the entire Southeast. He has been working in the adventure industry for over 30 years. He is currently an Associate Professor at North Carolina State University, specializing in adventure recreation, outdoor leadership, and park and protected area management. He has over 20 seasons as a Course Director and Instructor at the North Carolina Outward Bound School. He is a member of the NCOBS Board, where he chairs the safety committee, and participates in safety and program reviews for various organizations and the Association for Experiential Education.

Joe Forrester sent an e-mail this year asking if he could be of help in producing the publication. Given his background, he was put into service as a copy editor, which has been a great addition to the team. He has been a member of the American Alpine Club since 2004 and has climbed in many locales both domestically and abroad. He is the Senior Editor for the *Colorado College Alpine Journal* and has several peer-reviewed publications related to injury in the wilderness. He is currently a fourth-year medical student at the University of Virginia, and will be starting residency in general surgery at Stanford next year. Ultimately he plans to specialize in Trauma and Critical Care.

In addition to the dedicated individuals on the Safety Advisory Council, we are grateful to the following—with apologies for any omissions—for collecting data and for helping with the report: Hank Alacandri, Erik Hansen, Janet Miller, Leo Paik, Justin Preisendorfer, all individuals who sent in personal stories, and, of course, George Sainsbury.

John E. (Jed) Williamson
Managing Editor
7 River Ridge Road
Hanover, NH 03755
jedwmsn@mac.com

UNITED STATES

AVALANCHE, UNDERESTIMATED HAZARD, POOR POSITION
Alaska, Deltas, Canwell Glacier

About mid-day on February 27, we (author and two others) parked at Miller Creek and began skinning up through sustained high winds towards the terminus of the Canwell Glacier. While skinning on the flat river valley, occasional "whoomphing" was heard and remarked about with casual interest. At one point a very large portion of the snowpack settled, forming a crack that was visible in the horizontal snowpack. As we made our way up-valley, we began to speculate about an objective. There wasn't a lot of snow on the ridges bordering the glaciers, so we easily settled on the one part of the slope that actually had reasonable snow-cover, on the south side of the ridge separating the Canwell from the Fels Glacier.

As we approached, we realized that the slope was steeper than it looked, and one of us remarked that it looked dangerous and might not be a good idea to ski. But time for the ski was running short, and we just decided to go skin up for one hour and have a look at the slope more carefully. We agreed we would choose our route on an intermediate ridge, and the expectation was that good route choices would allow us to travel safely.

We arrived at the terminus of the Canwell Glacier and started skinning up towards the ridge on our north side. The base of the slope was covered by a 70-cm thick, very loose, powdery snow-cover, which had some depth-hoar at the base. It was basically skinning up on nothing and a few times the skis touched rocks on our way up. It was very, very difficult to skin up. Only the fact that the three of us have been doing ski-alpinism for years made us continue. I would not, under any circumstance, skin up that slope if I was a beginner.

About 50–80 meters up from the valley bottom, the snow was settled, way harder, and easier to skin on. In places it was sufficiently steep and hard that it was difficult to keep an edge in while skiing, and switchback turns became more challenging as the skis slid out from beneath. As we continued up, we became impressed about how much "whoomphing" we were encountering beneath the very hard snow surface, but reasoned that the snow was not very deep ("not deep enough to kill you"), and the unstable snow was probably in isolated pockets, so we continued up. We were all equipped for avalanche rescue and all the team had a pretty good idea on what to do in case of avalanche. Sinister noises were warning us.

Before we got to our turn-around time, there was only one last steep face to cross. Up there probably it was steeper (approaching 45 degrees). We recognized that this cone needed extra caution and we proposed to get it done one at the time. About 30 seconds later, the wind slab fractured

3

completely and began to avalanche. The slab cut loose about 100 to 150 meters above the top of our party. The snow broke in hard-edged, tabular blocks—consistent with the hard wind-slab we had been skinning up. The avalanche was perhaps 100 to 150 meters wide and encompassed more than the entire slope we had been traveling up.

Two of us were caught on the sides of the avalanche and got carried down with it, including one of us who thought he was safe on a little rocky knob sticking out of the slab. One of us was fully immersed in the slide and got carried down about 100 meters.

The avalanche was probably not powerful enough to rotate the person during its travel and carry the person all the way down. This person, however, disappeared from view and got into the avalanche, but it let him out after ten seconds. The two remaining team members were ready to perform a beacon search, but the avalanche had released him right when confusion started becoming fear because he realized that he could not breathe or move in it. A lot of snow in his mouth, a ski pole broken, and a bruised body.

After the avalanche, we teamed up again and we skied down one at the time over the slope covered by the avalanche.

Analysis

We are friends from work and are reasonably experienced backcountry skiers. All have taken avalanche safety courses and would say that we know how to identify dangerous avalanche conditions and pick safe routes through the snowy mountains. The conditions were not good. It was not a day for ski-alpinism. Lack of wise judgment and strong underestimation of the hazard did the rest. It looked like there was just enough snow to ski up there, and indeed for Alpine standards, it was a poorly covered slope. We had many warnings. But it took one of us getting fully swept away for us to turn around.

We think our experience shows that being well educated and experienced in the outdoors does not make you safe. To be safe, you also need to be sufficiently engaged to take responsibility for your own actions and position in the mountains. We strongly encourage everyone who goes in to the mountains to think and speak for yourselves, be critical and examining of your surroundings, and to follow your gut instincts. Do not surrender your personal responsibility for safety to the rest of the group. (Source: Did not want names in report)

HAPE, ASCENDING TOO FAST
Alaska, Mount McKinley, West Buttress

An eight-member expedition climbed from 7,200 feet to 14,200 feet in three days via the West Buttress. On May 14, eight days after the start of their climb, the expedition arrived at the 17,200-foot camp. Soon after their arrival, one of the members (45) expressed to his expedition members that he "felt tired." On May 17, two members of the expedition were encountered at the NPS rescue cache attempting to obtain oxygen from the NPS medical cache. Mountaineering Ranger Tucker Chenoweth asked if they needed medical assistance. They indicated they need assistance because one of their team members was "sick."

NPS Rangers responded with medical supplies and oxygen to the tent of the reported sick climber, who was found supine in his sleeping bag complaining of feeling disoriented and lethargic. A detailed patient exam was conducted finding: a heart rate of 129; respirations of 16; fine crackles in both of his lower lung lobes; a blood-oxygen saturation (SaO_2) of 50%; and ataxia when trying to walk. Patient was treated for high altitude pulmonary edema (HAPE) using oxygen therapy, albuterol, and nifedipine. Poor weather conditions prevented immediate evacuation. It was decided to continue treatment and monitor him throughout the night. Preparations were made on the evening of May 17 in anticipation for a technical lowering the following day.

At 0700 on May 18, the climber's condition remained stable. When taken off oxygen, his SPO_2 quickly returned to 40%. Due to the limited supply of oxygen, it was decided that immediate evacuation was necessary.   Weather conditions remained poor preventing any possibility of a helicopter evacuation. As a result, a 2,500-foot technical lowering operation was initiated at 1330. By 1500, the technical lower was complete and care was transferred to an NPS ground team who evacuated him the remaining distance by means of ski toboggan to the 14,200-foot medical tent.

The patient's condition resolved at the 14,200-foot camp where he was released to his remaining expedition members and descended under his own power.

Analysis

The eight member expedition climbed from 7,200 feet to 14,200 feet in three days. According to the affected climber, he had very little experience with high altitude climbing. The other seven members of his team had all climbed at elevations above 16,000 feet. They had the experience necessary to recognize the early symptoms associated with altitude illness. A three-day ascent to 14,200 feet is dangerously fast. It may have been appropriate for some of the members of this expedition to ascend this quickly, but not for all of them. Although it is nearly impossible to predict if someone will develop altitude illness, a quick ascent dramatically increases the odds. As a result of their quick ascent and disregard for early symptoms of altitude illness, the climber was unable to descend under his own power or with the help of his team. This required a difficult and potentially dangerous NPS rescue.

FALL ON SNOW, UNABLE TO SELF-ARREST, CLIMBING UNROPED, POOR POSITION
Alaska, Mount McKinley, Kahiltna Glacier

On May 16, French mountaineer Pascal Frison (51) fell to his death while climbing Mount McKinley. He and his partner were approaching a feature at the top of Motorcycle Hill known as "Lunch Rocks" near 12,000 feet on the West Buttress when Frison lost control of his sled, which he had untethered. In an attempt to stop it from sliding over the ridge, both Frison and his sled tumbled towards the Peters Glacier. Frison, who was unroped at the time, was unable to self-arrest and ultimately fell over 1,000 feet to a steep, crevassed section of the Peters Glacier.

A nearby team witnessed the fall and made a radio distress call shortly after 3:00 p.m. to the Denali National Park Rangers. At the time of the notification, the park's high altitude A-Star B3 helicopter was at the 14,200-foot camp on a re-supply flight. Within five minutes, the helicopter flew to the accident site with two mountaineering rangers on board as spotters. They saw several pieces of fallen gear and followed the fall line down to what appeared to be the climber lying in a crevasse around 10,200 feet.

As the steep terrain at the fall site offered no feasible landing areas, the helicopter and crew flew back to the Kahiltna Basecamp at 7,200 feet. After a two-man communications team was inserted at the top of the Peters Glacier, the A-Star B3 helicopter then returned to the crevasse site with NPS mountaineering ranger Kevin Wright on the end of a "short-haul" (end of a 120-foot rope). Wright could not safely reach the climber who was lying an additional 20-feet below him in the crevasse. However, Wright readily determined that the climber had not survived the long fall.

Analysis

In an expedition environment, equipment, supplies, and your life are very closely intertwined if not inseparable. It is understandable that Frison would have been in a very bad situation without his equipment, but he would not have lost his life. One cannot speculate whether the decision to jump onto a moving sled at the edge of such exposed terrain was a lack of sound judgment and/or an error in perception—or perhaps a reactionary instinct that was not driven by thought or strategy at all. Had Frison been roped up, the rope would have likely have stopped him from falling. Or perhaps it might have dragged both team members down the slope had he pursued the sled towards the edge.

Runaway sleds on Denali are a common occurrence. Most of these instances are a result of a momentary lapse of thought or a careless act. During pre-trip planning, we recommend developing a redundant rigging and attachment system and having a firm understanding of how to prevent a loaded sled from leaving you once on the mountain. (Source: Brandon

Latham, Mountaineering Ranger and Denali National Park and Preserve
News Report)

HAPE and HACE, ASCENDING TOO FAST
Alaska, Mount McKinley, West Buttress

After a rapid ascent to 14,200 foot camp on the West Buttress, a member of
the "Polish Female Denali 2010" expedition, Zygmunt Berdychowski (49),
began experiencing signs and symptoms of both High Altitude Pulmonary
Edema (HAPE) and High Altitude Cerebral Edema (HACE).

On the morning of May 24 at 0700, Dariusz Stolarczyk, the expedition
team leader, woke up hearing irregular respiratory sounds and recognized
signs of an altered mental status from Berdychowski. At 0900 Stolarczyk
approached the NPS Rangers requesting assistance for his team member.
Due to Berdychowski's inability to walk unassisted, Ranger Brandon Latham,
VIP Scott Ring and VIP Sam Piper moved Berdychowski in a litter to the
medical tent at 14,200-foot Ranger Camp. Berdychowski was treated at the
medical tent and evacuated on the NPS helicopter to basecamp and then
accompanied by a VIP paramedic to Talkeetna on a commercial fixed wing
aircraft. He was released at that point.

Analysis

The primary issue with this incident is the time the expedition took to ascend
to 14,200 feet. By using the old mountaineering philosophy of "Climb High,
Sleep Low," it would take a recommended five to seven days to ascend to
14,200 feet. Climbers who follow this philosophy may still experience symptoms of Acute Mountain Sickness (AMS), HAPE or HACE, but it is more
likely to happen to those who choose a more rapid ascent. Berdychowski
may have been able to increase his chances for proper acclimatization and
avoid the need to be evacuated if his team had planned a slower ascent up
to 14,200 feet. (Source: Brandon Latham, Mountaineering Ranger)

FALL ON ROCK, CLIMBING ALONE and UNROPED, PLACED NO PROTECTION
Alaska, Mount McKinley, West Rib

On May 26, solo climber Luc Benoit (40) sustained an un-roped fall of
approximately 1000 feet down the West Rib. The next day Ranger Tucker
Chenoweth flew with pilot Andy Hermansky in the contract A-star B3 helicopter 3AE to the scene and picked up the climber using a toe-in landing.
Benoit was assessed at basecamp by a Park Service volunteer physician,
flown to Talkeetna and released from NPS care.

Luc Benoit came to Denali with the intention of climbing the West Rib
solo. This was his third attempt at the route with previous experience as a
client of a guide service in 2006 and another try with a partner in 2009. He
reached the summit of Denali via the West Buttress in 2009, but had never

previously set foot on the lower West Rib. Before arriving in Alaska, Benoit had climbed solo in Bolivia on peaks above 20,000 feet. He intended to use these climbs to acclimatize for Denali.

After flying into basecamp on the Kahiltna glacier on May 22, Benoit moved up the lower West Rib according to his planned schedule. On May 26, Benoit left his highest camp at the top of the couloir, following footprints towards the "Upper West Rib camp." He reported snowy conditions to the first bergschrund, then reported that conditions got icy. He decided to climb through a mixed rock section. While attempting this, his ice ax "lost its grip" on the rock and he fell over backwards onto the "50–55-degree" slope. He rolled and slid on the snow between rocks then onto a snow slope, passing over the bergschrund. He came to rest in a sitting position, "face up in the direction of the mountain." When he tried to move, he noticed pain in his right shoulder. He also found that his tent and ice ax were lost in the fall. He descended to the couloir camp, dug a trench for shelter, and went to sleep for the night. Around 0800 on May 27, he called for Ranger assistance with his FRS radio and reached Ranger Tucker Chenoweth at basecamp.

Benoit was flown to basecamp, where a physician assessed him, finding injuries to his shoulder and ankle. Benoit then joined Ranger Dave Weber on a K2 flight back to Talkeetna. He refused additional medical care or transfer.

Analysis

Solo climbing always carries greater inherent risks and requires a much higher level of self-sufficiency. The West Rib route has significant objective hazard with a highly crevassed approach up the Northeast fork of the Kahiltna glacier as well as steep technical climbing with the possibility of very large falls. Most climbing parties use running protection on the steeper slopes starting at the main couloir at the base of the West Rib. Given the conditions present on May 26, snow pickets, ice screws, and rock protection would have been standard accepted practice to climb the route with a roped group. Solo climbing makes placing protection and self-belaying much more difficult, to the point where it would be nearly impossible to protect the route in the event of falls.

All climbing requires constant risk assessment in relation to the climber's ability and comfort level. It is common for solo climbers to set up ropes on steep and technical portions of climbs. If solo climbers choose to travel unroped, they risk being killed in the event of any slip or fall. (Source: Kevin Wright, Mountaineering Ranger)

AVALANCHE
Alaska, Denali National Park, Werewolf/Hut Towers, Freezy Nuts

On May 24, four members of an expedition were flown on to the Ruth Glacier with the intent to climb several surrounding snow and ice routes. Weather conditions in the area (4,500 feet) were unseasonably warm, with nighttime temperatures consistently above freezing. Over the next several days, the team made early morning attempts on the Japanese Couloir of Mount Barille and the West Ridge of Mount Dickey. In both cases, they aborted their climb because of signs of rapid warming in the snowpack. Because of the unfavorable climbing conditions, two members of the team elected to fly out on May 28, two days before their scheduled pick up. Canadians Andrew Herzenberg (39) and Israeli Avner Magen (42) opted to stay in and make an attempt on "Freezy Nuts," a 2500-foot snow and ice gully between the Werewolf and Hut Towers.

First climbed in 1996, this route is widely considered an up-and-coming classic because of its easy approach and relatively moderate climbing. The route is very narrow (less than ten feet wide) for about 1,500 feet and has a steep 600-foot headwall. The route is exposed to hanging snow and ice on adjacent rock walls. According to past trip reports, an average time for a team to ascend and descend this route is about 12–15 hours.

According to other climbers camped nearby, the pair left camp to begin their ascent just before 0100 on May 29. Photographs recovered from a camera show 6–12 inch boot penetration during their ascent of the lower portion of the route, indicating that early morning temperatures had not allowed for a surface freeze.

Sometime in the early afternoon on May 29 a climber also camped in the Ruth Gorge area, witnessed a "sizable" avalanche come down the "Freezy Nuts" gully. Unaware of the deceased pair's exact plans, the reporting climber only became concerned when they did not return to their tent by that evening. The reporting climber decided to ski across the glacier to where he could see the debris cone at the base of the gully and noticed what appeared to be scattered equipment and possibly a body. At 2056, the climber spoke with NPS staff in Talkeetna via satellite phone and reported his concerns.

At 2220, two NPS ranger staff departed Talkeetna via helicopter to pick up the reporting climber and investigate the incident site. Upon arrival, two bodies were immediately spotted, both on the surface and along the leading edge of a relatively small debris cone. The helicopter was able to land safely at the toe of the debris to within 100 feet of the bodies and rangers were able to exit the aircraft and confirm the two climbers' deaths.

Due to the late hour, the helicopter and crew returned to Talkeetna that night. The bodies and equipment were recovered the following morning via NPS helicopter and were transferred to the State of Alaska Medical Examiner in Talkeetna.

Analysis

Although "Freezy Nuts" is slowly gaining a reputation as a classic moderate snow and ice gully, it is an extremely recessed and narrow route subject to substantial objective hazards, particularly in poor weather conditions, such as after new snow or during warmer temperatures. Much of the route acts a funnel for sliding snow or falling debris.

Beginning on May 24, many climbing parties in the Ruth Glacier area reported a rapid warming trend and subsequently altered their climbing objectives. According to the deceased pair's climbing partners, they were concerned about the snow conditions before their climb on May 29. They chose to mitigate the hazards by climbing during the coldest hours and, according to a short audio clip recovered from Avner Magen's camera, they seemed prepared to turn around at any point. Although it is impossible to say exactly what ensued during their ascent, the end result is that they fell to the bottom of the climb while descending. The last of their photographs showed them about midway down the climb, one belaying the other down-climbing. Their ropes were found attached to one of the climbers, rigged for rappel. It is possible that either a fall occurred, or that a rappel anchor failed, and that the avalanche that occurred was the result of, or even secondary to their fall. However, given the weather history and the signs of instability in the area, it is likely that an avalanche caused the fall. The debris cone at the base of the gully was one of several cones that had likely occurred over the past week. Each of these avalanches can be characterized as having a relatively small destructive force and small to medium dimensions; however, because of the large vertical fall of the debris, the consequence of being carried is very high. This particular avalanche may be characterized as WL-U-R3-D2: a wet loose-snow avalanche, unknown trigger, medium size relative to its path, and small relative to its destructive potential.

It is not clear when Herzenberg started climbing mountains, but Magen was an accomplished mountaineer and chronicled his climbs from all over the world on his website. This was their first climbing trip in the Alaska Range. According to their climbing partners, they both had some experience with ice climbing and mountaineering.

Although it's difficult to conclude the exact cause of their accident, it is safe to say that the warm conditions on May 29 gave them a smaller margin of safety. (Source: Mik Shain, Mountaineering Ranger)

(Editor's Note: In a press release by Raveena Aulakh from the "Toronto Star," we learned something about these two men, information not normally found in official reports:

"On Monday, shocked friends and colleagues in Toronto [date unknown] were trying to come to terms with the loss of two men described as 'brilliant.' 'It's a very tough time for everyone in the department,' said Craig Boutilier, chair of the U. of Toronto computer science department where Magen was an associate professor. 'One thing to know about Avner is that he was a fantastic researcher... The stuff that he researched wasn't esoteric but was very deep theoretically,' said Boutilier.

"In another corner of the city, Herzenberg's colleagues at laboratory medicine and pathobiology department in the Faculty of Medicine at University Health Network were trying to understand the sequence of events. 'He was dedicated to research in kidney pathology, he was very generous as a collaborator with other physicians and scientists and he was an excellent teacher,' Richard Hegele, chair of the department, said of the assistant professor. 'He enthusiastically participated in training of new generations of specialists.'

"Both faculties have set up tribute pages on the departments' websites.")

FALL ON ICE/ROCK, PROTECTION PULLED OUT, PLACED INADEQUATE PROTECTION
Alaska, Mount McKinley, Cassin Ridge

On June 7, Belgian climber Joris Van Reeth of Borgerhout (27) was killed in a fall while climbing the Cassin Ridge. He was leading a highly techni-cal section of the route known as the Japanese Couloir when his anchor appeared to fail and he fell 100 feet in rocky terrain. Van Reeth fell to the approximate elevation of his partner Sam Van Brempt (24). Van Brempt was not injured, and after confirming that his friend had died in the fall, he used his satellite phone to call Denali National Park rescue personnel.

A climbing ranger was flown in the park helicopter to Van Brempt's lo-cation at the 13,000-foot level to assess the terrain for a possible shorthaul rescue and recovery, although fog and clouds moved in before a rescue could be performed. While on the reconnaissance flight, the ranger had observed a second, unrelated team climbing on the route several hundred feet below the Belgian party. According to Van Brempt, who called back via satellite phone later that night, two Japanese climbers reached him in the early evening and assisted Van Brempt in lowering Van Reeth's body down to a safer location just above the Northeast Fork of the Kahiltna Glacier at 11,500 feet.

Denali National Park rescue personnel took advantage of a break in the clouds to evacuate Sam Van Brempt from the base of the Cassin Ridge late Thursday night June 10. (Source: Denali Park and Preserve News Releases, Maureen McLaughlin)

Analysis

Examination of the photos taken of the accident revealed only two pieces of rock protection (a cam and a stopper) still clove hitched to the ropes. There were no ice screws. The last piece of ice protection would have been approximately 20 meters below his last stance. This explains why a long leader fall was taken. The actual location of his last anchor position is unknown so it cannot be determined with absolute certainty why his rock protection failed.

The most probable scenario is that the cam and stopper were in the same crack and that the cam levered the flake apart, releasing both pieces of rock pro. The second possibility is that there was ice coating the inside of the crack. When pressure was placed on the pieces they slowly melted out and released suddenly. The helmet was recovered but no damage or blood was found on the shell and chin strap assembly. This suggests that the helmet was either not being worn or the chinstrap was not secured during the time of the fall. (Source: John Loomis, Mountaineering Ranger)

FALL ON SNOW – SKI MOUNTAINEERING
Alaska, Mount McKinley, West Buttress

On June 28 at 1315, a climber (32) fell while skiing down from the fixed lines on the way to the 14,200-foot camp. National Park Service Ranger Dave Weber and a Volunteer-In-Parks doctor watched as the climber fell towards the bottom of his run. He fell forward while moving at a high velocity and a sudden deceleration brought him to an abrupt halt in the snow. Due to the fact that the skier was ambulatory very soon after the fall, NPS personnel did not respond immediately to the scene. At 1400, one of the climber's partners reported, "He thinks that he broke a rib." His partners were instructed to assist the climber from their tent to the NPS medical tent.

The patient assessment care report (PCR) notes pleuritic left focal anterior rib pain and vital signs within normal limits (except an elevated blood pressure, of which the patient had a history). Due to the fact that the NPS helicopter was in close proximity on another mission, the climber was continuously monitored to determine whether an evacuation would be required. Although he did not exhibit any signs or symptoms of an underlying lung injury, concerns about the possibility of a pneumothorax prompted continued assessment. Later that afternoon it was determined that an evacuation would be necessary and this information was relayed to Talkeetna.

During a resupply flight that afternoon, the climber was loaded into the helicopter and flown to the 7,200-foot camp. He was released to return to Talkeetna via an awaiting taxi service plane.

Analysis

The potential for a life-threatening injury was the justification for the air evacuation of the climber from the 14,200-foot camp. This evacuation emphasizes an important point concerning rescues facilitated by the NPS on Denali. Due to the remote and dynamic mountain environment, evacuation decision-making differs markedly from that in the 911 emergency system. The risks involved with rescue operations, including air evacuation, from 14,200 feet, although manageable, can never be negated. It is for this reason that we do not utilize these resources before careful scrutiny. It is always prudent to make evacuation decisions based on likely scenarios and the information gathered during on-going patient assessments. However, there are times that due to weather, resource availability, and other external factors, decisions must be made based on the possibility of the worst-case scenario unfolding. (Source: David Weber, Mountaineering Ranger)

(Editor's Note: There were a number of medical issues on Denali this year. These were not considered "accidents" because they did not happen as a result of climbing. The HAPE and HACE cases that happened because of ascending too rapidly, however, are counted—and reported on—though not all appear in the narratives above. The medical episodes included several separate guided clients and two non-guided climbers developing AMS and then HAPE signs and symptoms after a normal ascent time; and a 55-year-old client with a previous history of a kidney stone who experienced severe abdominal pain. All these resulted in evacuation from the mountain.)

BEE SWARM – STRANDED
Arizona, Mount Lemon

On August 11, a rock climber was stung more than 1,000 times when he and his three partners encountered a beehive about 6:30 p.m. and were attacked atop Mount Lemmon.

His partners were able to escape the swarm, but he was stranded for several hours. Search and rescue crews were able to rescue him about 9:15 p.m. after rappelling down to his location.

The four climbers suffered more than 1,300 bee stings, with the stranded climber suffering more than 1,000 stings. Three of the four were hospitalized. (Source: Edited from a posted report by Brian Pederson, on the *Arizona Daily Star* site)

(Editor's Note: It has been a few years since the last report of bees being encountered by climbers. Bees are a common hazard in some climbing areas, so it is good to check with locals and/or land managers before climbing.)

ROCKFALL, FALL ON ROCK, BELAYER LOST CONTROL WHEN STRUCK BY ROCK
Arizona, Prescott National Forest, Granite Mountain

On December 12, Elise Anderson (21), Jeff Rome (21), and Chris Shanehoffer (26), went to climb at Granite Mountain. Their route for the day was Granite Jungle—two pitches of 5.6 leading into the third pitch of Chieu Hoi—5.9. They started their hour and a half hike to the base of the cliff at 0730. They left their packs at an open ledge called the "Front Porch" and scrambled the 300-meter climber trail to the base of the route.

Elise chose to lead the first pitch, as she had previously followed it. She protected the bottom of the pitch with two evenly spaced pieces of gear. About 40 feet above the base, she assessed a large block wedged in the crack and chose to sling it as natural pro for her third protection point. (Local climbers attest to testing, pulling, and standing on this block in the past. It is a prominent route feature known as The Horn.)

As she moved up, the block, about 80 pounds, dislodged, striking her laterally on her upper left leg and caused her to fall. The rock then struck a ledge at the base, broke into two parts and struck Jeff, the belayer, who sustained minor injuries to his arm and hip. At this point, Jeff lost control of the belay (a belay plate) and Elise continued falling for a total of 35 feet, stopping just above a sharp block at the base of the route. She was caught by her top gear placement, the second piece.

The rope was de-sheathed between Elise and her belay. Most likely the rock that dislodged also struck her rope and partially cut it. It is likely that the de-sheathed rope somehow jammed in a carabiner because Jeff remembers Elise hanging from her harness a few feet above the ground and he did not have his hands on the brake strand of the rope.

Chris assisted Elise to the base as Jeff ran back to get his cell phone from the packs. He called 911 at 0935 and teams from Central Yavapai Fire and Prescott City Fire were deployed. Three climbing parties, which included a surgeon, a WFR/climbing instructor, another WFR, and me (a WEMT/climbing instructor), were spread out on the approach trail at the time of the accident. All three teams ran into Jeff running down to the trailhead to lead rescue teams up the complex approach trail.

I arrived on scene at 1030 and assessed that Elise had not lost consciousness and did not have head, neck or spinal trauma/pain or signs of neural deficit. Her vitals were normal, and she was not exhibiting signs and symptoms of shock an hour after the fall. She had abrasions on her hands, rope burn on her left shoulder, and a swollen and deformed left ankle. She complained of severe pain in her upper left leg and when I exposed the leg, an obvious deformity indicated a mid-shaft femur fracture. No other injuries were identified.

Since the leg injury was closed with no bruising or signs of distal blood loss, I removed a tourniquet that had been placed by the first party on scene and began removing Elise's gear to prepare her for a litter carry to an appropriate extrication point. We were waiting for a traction splint and a litter to arrive with the SAR teams and we determined that the Front Porch would be the most obvious extrication point for air evacuation, as loose blocks above the accident site were identified as a hazard for the patient and rescuers.

At 1130 Chief Cougan Carothers (Central Yavapai Fire) was the first of the rescue personnel to arrive and took over as field commander for this operation. We cleared a trail through thick brush for the litter carry to the Front Porch, and set anchors for belays and lowers through technical steps. By 1400 Elise was short-hauled in a Bauman Bag (a single-point suspension for hoisting a patient), then transferred to an air ambulance and flown to Flagstaff Medical

Center. She had sustained a broken femur and a broken ankle. She has had two successful surgeries and is expected to have a full recovery.

Analysis

All three had previously climbed together and had done this route and other Granite Mountain routes. They were all competent at basic rock climbing skills and had all received formal training in rock climbing.

Climbing at any area puts us at risk of rockfall. The climbing party involved did many things correctly. Elise and Jeff were both wearing helmets, which is, unfortunately, not the norm at this climbing area. While belaying, Jeff was positioned to the side of the direct rockfall zone (which may have saved his life), and the team had a cell phone. By positioning the belay to the side and not anchoring himself, however, he was pulled upward from his stance, and this pull in combination with being struck by the rock caused him to let go of the belay. A ground anchor and appropriate belay stance in this case would have mitigated these hazards.

Though it is not common for climbers to use auto-locking devices on multi-pitch routes, a belay device such as a GriGri or Cinch would have shortened Elise's fall.

Emergency response teams would have responded differently and brought different tools (traction splint) had they known the injury was a broken femur. Jeff informed the 911 dispatcher that Elise had broken the tibia and fibula rather than the femur. A good lesson from this incident is to take the time to gather accurate and detailed information and to report it carefully to the dispatcher. It was helpful that most of the people on scene were trained in wilderness medicine, as this facilitated a smooth and calm rescue operation. Climbers on scene integrated well with rescue teams as a result of these skills.

If a rescue litter had been cached at this popular climbing area, it is likely that with the resources and people on scene, an immobilization and carry of the patient to the Front Porch (300 meters) would have been feasible one hour after the accident took place. This may have allowed a helicopter evacuation to be initiated upon the arrival of rescue personnel and cut the total rescue time by more than half. (The litter that was hiked up did not arrive on scene until three and a half hours after the accident).

We learned during the rescue that a litter had been cached at the Front Porch for an event such as this. (Chief Carothers had stopped to look for it, since he thought it was still cached.) The litter was cached several years ago in response to another accident and prior to the designation of Granite Mountain as a wilderness area. It was removed by Prescott College in 2009 after discussions with the Prescott National Forest Wilderness Manager, as it was thought to be old and unsafe and not in compliance with the U.S. Forest Service wilderness management policy. A review of this policy or replacement of the cached litter with a modern litter was not deemed necessary at that time. Had Elise's femur fracture involved major arteries, or if her injuries had been more serious, a cached litter could have served as the difference between life and death. In light of this accident, local rescue and climber groups are appealing to the Prescott N.F. wilderness managers to replace the cached litter. This raises the issue of reviewing management policy regarding life safety at wilderness climbing areas across the country. (Sources: Climbers involved in the accident and rescue efforts, Chief Cougan Carothers, Central Yavapai Fire, Prescott National Forest, and David Lovejoy, Adventure Education Program, Prescott College. This report was compiled by Viren Perumal, WEMT, AMGA Rock Guide, Prescott College Instructor, and edited by John Dill and Jed Williamson)

FALL ON ROCK, SLACK ROPE
Arkansas, Horseshoe Canyon Ranch

My wife Kylie and I (age unknown) were climbing at Horseshoe Canyon Ranch near Jasper on December 22. I was going to lead Frankenberry (5.9+), a six-bolt route approximately 60 feet in length. The crux was just under the third bolt with a small technical roof. I made it to the third bolt located at the top of the roof. In order to clip the third bolt I had to climb above it, reach down, and make the clip.

Out of habit I said, "clipping," before making the clip. Kylie reacted by giving me slack, but this time being above the bolt I didn't need any more slack since I had more slack than I needed from the second to the third bolt, and slack about two feet above the third bolt, and the slack my belayer just gave me to clip in with.

On my way to make the clip with my left hand, my right hand slipped and I fell. At the bottom of the route was a four feet wide by two feet high rectangular shaped boulder. About two feet above the boulder, Kylie started to catch me, but due to the slack, it was too late. Mid-way through the stretch of the rope, I hit the boulder heels first and then the rope snapped tight. With Kylie in the air, I began screaming for help. Luckily, three climbers came to our rescue and helped Kylie down. My first thought was that I had broken my back, but after lying there for about ten minutes, I realized my heels hurt more than anything. We were able to walk out and drive to the hospital. The damage: I broke the top-outside of my right foot, my left ankle, and cracked my left heel. I also bruised the bottoms of both my feet and my back.

Analysis

Be aware of how much slack you have out. It's both the climber and belayer's responsibility to monitor this. Anchoring the belayer may have also helped prevent this misadventure, especially when there's a big difference in weight. (Source: Edited from a post on www.rockclimbing.com.)

CLIMBER CAUSED FRACTURE OF ICE DAM RESULTING IN FALLING WATER AND FALL ON ICE, CLIMBING UNROPED, INADEQUATE PROTECTION, WEATHER, EXPOSURE
California, Lee Vining Canyon

On February 16, Christy McIntire (31) and Victor Lawson (37) were ice climbing in Lee Vining Canyon, just east of Tuolumne Meadows. They began their day of climbing on Main Wall, a popular area for ice climbers in the eastern Sierra. After topping out Main Wall on a WI4 multi-pitch route, they discovered an enticing smaller wall of ice, roughly one pitch long and WI2 at it's steepest. As they approached the flow, both McIntire and Lawson deemed it safe to climb without a rope given their collective experience and comfort on ice in this difficulty range. With the rope and packs left at the base, they began to ascend the snowfield towards the ice wall. Staggered horizontally about fifteen feet apart and Lawson ten feet above, McIntire and Lawson started climbing the less than vertical ice confidently.

Lawson was the first to reach the top of the ice wall. As he swung in his right tool into the most prominent part of the top of the ice, which ended the steep section of ice, he instantly heard a "Velcro ripping" sound. He watched as two huge fracture lines split out from his pick and met after forming a "body-sized" plug of ice that "hovered for a split second" before being blown out and down by a surge of water. Lawson recounts how the ice almost "bubbled up and blew a part like a blister," releasing a ton of water and ice. Broken ice and water gushed out and fell down onto McIntire, who was still ten feet short of the top out. The three-foot wave of water, thick with pieces of broken ice and slush, overtook McIntire and pushed her off the ice wall and down into the snowfield a total of eighty to a hundred feet. The fall was not clean. She hit rocks and bumps of ice, bruising and breaking her body. During the fall, McIntire lost her ice tools (she was climbing leash-less), which prevented her from making a self-arrest once she hit the snowfield at the base of the flow. Finally, after digging her limbs into the snow, she managed to stop before hitting a large talus field. Conscious but disorientated, McIntire began to crawl away fearing more debris may come down onto her. However, the fall had a rattling effect and McIntire, extremely disoriented, was actually only crawling in circles at the base of the ice wall.

Meanwhile, Lawson, who was unharmed, topped out and then down climbed easier terrain to reach her. McIntire performed a self-assessment and determined that she was severely injured and unable to walk, let alone stand. Not only was McIntire's body broken from the fall, but also she was completely damp from the surge of water. Concerned about hypothermia, she stripped off her wet outer layers and put on pieces of dry clothing from

Lawson. Lawson and McIntire employed several techniques to cover the difficult winter terrain. She was able to scoot on her backside for the steeper sections of the descent and be dragged by her daisy chain on her harness during the flatter parts of the descent with the help of Lawson. The descent back to their truck took over four hours (normally a 30 minute hike). Finally the pair reached the truck at 9:00 p.m. and contacted Northern Inyo Hospital in Bishop, where McIntire works as RN. She informed the ER staff of the accident and her need for immediate medical attention once they arrived to town. The drive took about an hour and a half. After being examined by doctors, McIntire's injuries from the accident were diagnosed as a concussion, a torn ACL, a torn medial and lateral meniscus, a tibial plateau fracture, two sprained ankles, a broken great toe, multiple contusions and small lacerations.

Analysis

You cannot control nature. Rocks break, ice will crack, snow can slide and water can fall. No matter the terrain and the level of experience of the climber, accidents can happen beyond any climber's control and it is the job of the climber to always use best judgment to keep themselves and their partner safe. Soloing is ALWAYS dangerous and it is important for a climber to be aware of the full risks to make the best decision of how they choose to climb. For McIntire and Lawson, this particular accident took place at the very end of the day when the pair was trying to squeeze in one last climb before the day ended. More attention to temperatures of the day and the recent week might have helped prevent the accident. Most importantly, knowledge and awareness of different ice climbing conditions may help prevent disasters. McIntire and Lawson, both experienced ice climbers, had never heard of an ice dam before the accident took place. Knowledge of such a force in their field of climbing might have made these climbers aware of this possibility.

For McIntire, climbing with her ice tools without leashes may have saved her life. Had her tools been leashed, they might have caused her to experienced deadly puncture wounds, causing the accident go from severe to fatal. Lawson also had no formal training in wilderness emergency response. In this case, common sense and McIntire's training as a RN helped them make smart choices, post accident.

If one intends to engage in outdoor adventure with potentially high consequences, it's highly recommended that they also become certified as a Wilderness First Responder, Emergency Medical Technician, or equivalent, and are up to date on self rescue skills. Ice climbing has many outside risk factors that can vary depending on temperature and weather conditions, requiring constant re-assessment and awareness of ice conditions and surroundings. (Source: Christy McIntire)

HACE, WEATHER
California, Mount Shasta Wilderness

Two experienced 26-year-old climbers (Mr. Thomas and Mr. Tom Bennett) were spending the weekend on the north side of Mount Shasta (very rarely used at this time of the year due to snow covered road access). They climbed the Bolam Glacier on March 26th and then the Whitney on March 27. They summited late and experienced extremely high winds in the summit plateau area. While they had experienced wind while climbing, they were somewhat sheltered by the terrain above the glacier. High winds and a lenticular cloud had formed in front of an approaching storm. The storm was not forecast to have much precipitation (compared to the norm on Mt. Shasta), but strong winds are common in front of a storm and behind it. The winds made it nearly impossible to stand, so they decided to dig a snow cave and descend at first light. They had good clothing, equipment and training to bivy overnight.

The following morning they decided to descend. The strong winds had decreased and visibility had improved. As they got ready to go, Tom Bennett began to experience problems with his vision and muscular control. He had a hard time putting on his crampons. As they began the descent, he was showing signs of ataxia and was quickly unable to walk. Mr. Thomas decided to return to the snow cave and call for help, which he did at 0848. His batteries were very weak in the cold weather. Unfortunately, deteriorating weather prevented assistance from the Siskiyou County SAR. Their route and trailhead were unknown until the USFS Law Enforcement found their vehicle on the north side.

Siskiyou County Sheriff SAR and the USFS Climbing Rangers set up a search base at the stranded climbers' vehicle on the north side of the mountain. Two USFS Climbing Rangers used snowmobiles to reach the trailhead area and continued up the route on skis. The winds were 40+ mph at 8000 feet. The Climbing Rangers stashed their skis and continued on foot until at 9000 feet, 60–70 mph winds prevented further travel. Visibility was extremely low. Mr. Thomas reached the Sheriff's SAR coordinator by phone (very weak battery) and said that he had descended and was following a creek. The Climbing Rangers descended and used the snowmobiles to search for tracks and found Mr. Thomas and transported him to the search base. At that point Mr. Thomas reported that he thought Mr. Bennett had suffered from HACE and that after they returned to the snow cave, Mr. Bennett lost consciousness and later appeared to have died. Mr. Thomas had attempted CPR, and when he realized that he had done everything he could with no results, Mr. Thomas decided to descend before his own condition worsened. He left food and water with Mr. Bennett, covered the opening to the cave with Mr. Bennett's backpack to protect him from high winds and snow, and marked the snow cave area with his avalanche probe. He descended in the latter part of the day, reaching the terminus of the Whitney Glacier in the dark and dug another snow cave for shelter (their base-camp was farther east). The following morning he continued his descent in high winds and low visibility and was eventually found by Climbing Rangers at a low elevation. High winds, snowfall, and poor visibility restricted the search for Mr. Bennett on Tuesday. On Wednesday the search base moved to the Weed Airport and California Highway Patrol and Cal Fire helicopters assisted in the search. Poor weather conditions (high winds and low visibility) limited flights and they were unsuccessful in inserting Climbing Rangers anywhere near the upper mountain. Thursday morning, April 1, a military Chinook helicopter (Cal Air Guard) was able to drop off three Climbing Rangers and two SAR members below the summit at 14,000 feet. The temperature was -10 F, winds were 20–30 mph and cloud cover began to increase. After extensive searching, they were able to find the rime-covered markers left by Mr. Thomas and eventually Mr. Bennett's body. The autopsy showed that Mr. Bennett had died of High Altitude Cerebral Edema (HACE).

Analysis
Both of the climbers involved had excellent equipment and several years of mountaineering experience. Illness was the immediate cause of this fatality. Weather the contributory cause.

Weather usually starts 6–12 hours earlier on the mountain than it does in town, with high winds and low visibility common. Although many people associate serious high altitude illness with higher elevations, both HACE and HAPE occur on Mt. Shasta, at 14,162 feet. From the description provided by Mr. Thomas, the early warning signs of altitude illness common with Acute Mountain Sickness (AMS), which can develop into HACE, were not noticed or reported, and Mr. Bennett deteriorated rapidly with HACE. (Source: Eric White, USFS Lead Climbing Ranger)

(Editor's Note: This was the only narrative from Mount Shasta, but the following is an edited summary of climbing accidents from Mount Shasta Wilderness:

Precipitation for the 2009/2010 winter was 121% of normal with the snow pack in May at 127% of normal. However, we experienced an extended winter as cool temperatures and wet weather continued into early June. These weather conditions caused late winter climbing conditions to extend into early summer, or as our neighbor Rainier National Park says, "an incubated winter." Smooth and firm snow on the routes, as well as thick rime ice on rock outcroppings, created greater risks than are normally experienced in June. As a result, a greater number of accidents than the past few years occurred. Climbing conditions remained in good shape through September.

There were 27 climbing accidents, nine of which were from rockfall and ten of which involved falling on snow or ice. Most rescues were conducted in Avalanche Gulch. Seventeen occurred on ascents, ten on descents. Thirteen climbers were exceeding their abilities. Injuries included 15 fractures, five sprains/strains, two concussions, and two back spasms/pain. Thanks to Eric White's Mount Shasta Wilderness Climbing Ranger Report)

FALL ON ROCK, INADEQUATE PROTECTION
California, Yosemite National Park, Middle Cathedral

On May 6, I took a lead fall way bigger than I would have liked and got to have a couple fun helicopter rides because of it. Just thought I'd share what happened so that others might learn second-hand rather than first-hand.

So Thursday afternoon, the reality of the day diverged greatly from the original agenda for the day. My climbing partner and I went to climb the East Buttress of Middle Cathedral in Yosemite, which is eleven pitches. There's one pitch of 5.10a (mixed) and the rest are 5.8 or easier trad.

Things had been going pretty well and at about 3:00 p.m. we were at the top of the 8th pitch, which I was leading. I'd been feeling comfy and confident all day. Didn't feel in over my head or sketched out. I was up about 120 feet from where my partner was belaying me and had stopped to look for a place to put in a piece of pro. The area was certainly protectable, but required a little looking around rather than a perfect crack to just jam cam after cam into. My previous piece was a Black Diamond 0.3 C4 cam about 10 or 12 feet below where I was looking, which seemed reasonable given the relatively easy terrain we were on. I never felt uneasy or precarious.

I don't remember slipping, and I don't remember falling the 35-foot distance to pro, which happily held, x 2 plus a little lead slack plus rope stretch. Apparently I smacked a little 8–12-inch ledge or some other part of the rock, because it knocked me out for what my climbing partner thinks was about 30 seconds.

I don't remember climbing back up to the little ledge and I don't remember setting up an anchor and clipping in to it. I have vague recollections of resting there to try to clear my head, checking the locked-ness of my 'biner several times and belaying my partner up to me.

After taking a bit of time to evaluate the situation and me asking my partner to check my anchor (apparently a few times), we decided that my obvious but unknown head injuries and back injuries made it too dangerous for us to go either up or down. Conveniently, Yosemite has a very well trained (and unfortunately often-used) Search and Rescue team very near. This is quite different from the normal alpine environment. My partner flipped through on one of our radios until she made contact with someone on the Nose who could get us help from below. We were put into direct radio contact with a guy from SAR, who checked on our whereabouts and condition and arranged for two SAR guys to climb up to us to meet us for a helicopter pick. It was great to be able to have constant contact with him.

When the SAR guys showed up, they quickly checked me out, checked out our anchor and gear situations, and noted that we were generally well prepared ;-). The helicopter showed up and dropped off the litter, they all got me loaded snugly into it, then got me clipped in to the haul-line when the helicopter returned, and off I flew down to the meadow below. All that took around three hours, which is ridiculously fast for getting a call out, a team organized, two guys up eight pitches of trad climbing, rescue gear dropped, rescue gear set up, and me picked up.

At the meadow I was transferred to a medic helicopter and taken to the hospital in Modesto, where they told me that I had suffered a pretty decent concussion, a few fractured lumbar vertebrae, a few more bruised vertebrae in the upper back, some bruised ribs, and a whole bunch of general scrapes and bruises. Could have been way worse.

Analysis

We (myself, my partner, and our friends that came with us) have done quite a bit of talking about what happened to figure out what we could have done better, what we did well, etc. The things I would have done differently include setting up an autoblock or some other back-up on my belay for my partner—given the situation, calling for help more quickly, and not falling. I try to make a habit of not falling, especially on gear. My partner noted that the fall could have happened to anyone, and I apparently looked really solid up until that point. All it takes is just a second to take you off the rock. There's a fine line between being in your groove and being over-confident

We talked a lot about the spacing of gear, and all felt that the spacing seemed reasonable for the difficulty of the terrain and the limited amount of gear that anyone climbs with. I guess a few things to note are that eight-inch ledges can be dangerous just like three-foot ledges, that those ledges get "closer than they appear" given all the rope stretch, and that maybe our definitions of "reasonable" need to be adjusted.

Things that we think we did well included a number of things. One, both staying levelheaded and rational the entire time. Two, calling for help when help was available rather than putting ourselves further into harm's way. (In an alpine environment or one in which help is a less reasonable alternative, we would have been forced to begin planning a self-rescue. We seriously considered that option.) Three, carrying radios. Four, my partner's attentive belaying. Five, both carrying enough gear on our harnesses and in our follower-pack to deal with an unplanned emergency situation. (Even the SAR guys ended up borrowing a couple small things.) As my partner pointed out, half an hour later or a bit windier would have put us there for the night. They even at one point asked if we were equipped to stay the night. Six, wearing our frickin' helmets (which we always do anyway).

We both think that it's incredibly important to thoroughly analyze and evaluate our accident so that we can learn from it as best possible. We count ourselves as very lucky, but also have endeavored to stack the odds in our favor. The hard work, efforts, and risks taken by those that assisted us can never be understated. (Source Johanna Hingle, 28, from a posting on Mountainproject.com)

RAPPEL RIGGING ERROR – FALL ON ROCK, DISTRACTION
California, Yosemite Valley, Serenity Crack

On May 7, Brian Ellis (31) and Japhy Dhungana (25), his frequent climbing partner of several years, climbed Serenity Crack (three pitches, 5.10d) and Sons of Yesterday (five pitches, 5.10a), which starts at the top of Serenity. They began rappelling the routes using the Reepschnur method shown in the illustration, page 25. The climbing rope is passed through one or more rappel rings and knotted to a thin "retrieval" cord. The rappeller descends the single rope, supported by the knot jammed against the rings, while leaving the cord unloaded. In case the knot slips through the rings, a figure-of-eight loop is tied in the cord just below the rings and clipped to the rope on the rappeller's side of the rings with a locking carabiner, thus securing the system. After the rappel, the rope is retrieved by pulling the cord. Advantages of this method include the ability to use single-rope descent devices and the reduced weight of the second rope for full-length rappels.

Ellis used the Reepschnur method because he favored rappelling with his Trango Cinch, an auto-locking, single-rope belay device. He typically joined the rope and cord with a flat overhand bend—in which the rope ends point in the same direction—backed up by a secondary overhand. (Again, see illustration.) Usually Ellis would go first, and then Dhungana would rappel with both the rope and the cord rigged through his ATC. Since he was no longer dependent on the security of the knot-jam, Dhungana would first disconnect the carabiner and untie the figure-of-eight loop to minimize the risk of the rope hanging up when they retrieved it. On this they were using a 10.2-mm rope and a 6-mm cord.

At the top of pitch 3 of Serenity Crack, Ellis rigged the next rappel through two rappel rings while Dhungana organized the 6-mm cord and chatted with a climber leading the pitch below. Dhungana checked Ellis's rigging and then Ellis rappelled, carrying a bundle of the cord in his hand to keep it from tangling. After 20–30 feet, he stopped to photograph the climber as he led the crux section. He stayed there for about ten minutes, moved left and right for different photo angles, and then resumed his descent. Almost immediately he began to fall. Dhungana described it in an Internet post, "This is when I heard a pop and the sound of the rope whizzing. I tried to grab the [cord] with my bare hands and held on tightly as long as I could. My instinct even tried to wrap it around my waist for an emergency brake, but the [cord] just burned through my hand." The cord tangled and then jammed at the ring and the impact broke the cord. Ellis fell 300–400 feet to the ground. Dhungana called 911 and a medical team arrived within nine minutes but Ellis died at the scene.

Analysis

It turned out that both overhand knots had slipped through the rappel rings. The figure-of-eight and carabiner backup should have prevented further slippage, but Ellis had completely overlooked rigging the backup, so there was no figure-of-eight or carabiner in the system. (See illustration facing page.) When Ellis fell there was probably nothing Dhungana could have done to stop him. In Dhungana's post on the Internet he wrote, "When Brian set up this system and tied the knots (I was coiling the ropes in the meantime preparing for tossing), he forgot to tie the backup knot. When I checked the system for him, I too, committed the same mistake and only observed the main knot. [Brian] checked it a THIRD time, and made the same oversight.

"The only explanation I have for this oversight is distraction and complacency. Brian MAY not have been 100% focused on the task (there were several things going on: party coming behind us and he was excited to take photos of the leader below; a few moments earlier on the last pitch, we were rudely and inconsiderately passed up by a speeding simul-climbing party, and this bothered both of us considerably). I am equally guilty of the same distraction and complacency for not having noticed the absence of the backup.

"During every [single-rope] rappel that Brian and I have done together with this system, we have tied the backup knot. The principle overhand knot had NEVER passed through the rings before. However, the one time [the backup figure-of-eight] was forgotten, sadly, was when it was most critical."

When examined after the accident, the primary overhand bend was compressed so much that it passed through the rings with room to spare. Much of the compression was probably due to the subsequent impact of the cord jamming, but Ellis's body weight plus his movements as he took pictures was enough to pull both knots through the rings, even with several strands of cord and webbing from the anchor competing for space. (The illustrations show the actual number of anchor strands, to scale.) These rings were the rolled aluminum type with 1½-inch interior diameter (ID). The ID on some welded stainless steel rings common on modern fixed anchors is smaller, but only by ⅛ inch—hardly enough insurance for a compressible/deformable material like a single knotted rope.

Several variations of the Reepschnur exist, with different characteristics and some with bigger knots, e.g., tying the figure-of-eight on a bight in the end of the rope rather than in the cord. If you're considering the Reepschnur, evaluate all the options and remember that you won't always find suitable anchor hardware in the mountains. If the second rappeller will use a two-rope descent

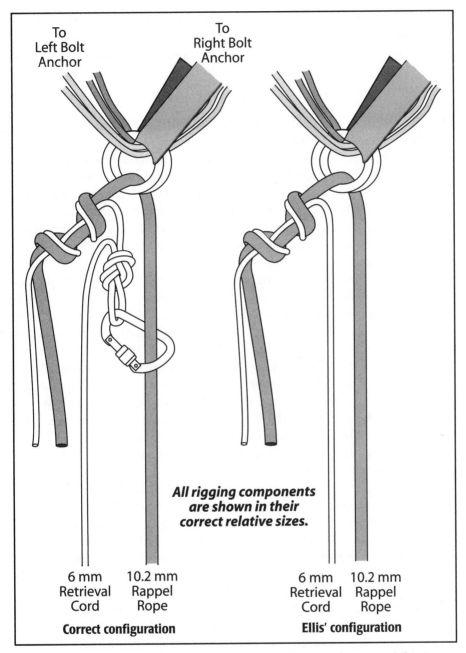

To
Left Bolt
Anchor

To
Right Bolt
Anchor

**All rigging components
are shown in their
correct relative sizes.**

6 mm	10.2 mm
Retrieval	Rappel
Cord	Rope

Correct configuration

6 mm	10.2 mm
Retrieval	Rappel
Cord	Rope

Ellis' configuration

device—which poses its own risks due to different strand sizes and friction—consider simply tying the single rope to the anchor for the first rappeller.

You might think it unlikely that two intelligent and experienced climbers working together could make the fatal mistakes described here. But ANAM is full of other cases, so before you put down this booklet and turn your attention elsewhere, remember that you have no way to distinguish Ellis or Dhungana from yourself until you retire from climbing and can say that it didn't happen to you. (Source: John Dill, NPS Ranger. Illustrations by Rick Weber. Special thanks to Japhy Dhungana for quickly posting his report to the climbing community.)

PROTECTION FAILURE – FALL ON ROCK, INADEQUATE PROTECTION
California, Yosemite, El Capitan

In May, Jean-Noel "Jano" Crouzat (48), an experienced French guide, was seriously injured while climbing the Salathé Wall (35 pitches, Grade VI) on El Capitan. The following account was written by his partner on the route, Thibaut "Tibo" Mauron, a member of the Swiss National Team. It has been translated from the original French and edited for ANAM, with bracketed text added by the editors for background. The story starts at Heart Ledges on their second day on the wall:

May 20: We woke up at day light around 6:30 a.m. I led the first pitches up to Hollow Flake Ledge. Jano led the 5.7 chimney, I led the next pitch and then Jano climbed smoothly to belay 19. It was 7:40 p.m. when we were done hauling pitch 19. It was a little late, but still plenty of time to make it to El Cap Spire, [the end of pitch 20], where we planned to sleep, and only one pitch left. We knew that two climbers were sleeping at the Alcove already [a bivy ledge 50 feet up pitch 20] and two were on El Cap Spire.

7:50 p.m: Jano started the lead and after 30 feet, I couldn't see him anymore because he was inside the Alcove. The climbers in the Alcove, John [an American guiding in Tasmania] and Anna [from Germany], were already inside their sleeping bags and having dinner. Jano chatted with them a little and then kept moving up.

Between the Alcove and the Spire there is a 75-foot chimney that is not too hard but not too protectable. Jano placed three pieces on the main wall and later placed another piece. Jano was holding the last piece he placed with one hand and the ledge on top of the Spire with the other hand and was talking with Stefan and Gerta, the two Austrian climbers already there. According to Stefan, that piece—a blue #3 Camalot supporting Jano, was not well placed. It failed, and Jano fell into the chimney, held by his next piece. I didn't hear anything, but felt the rope tighten. Anna and John didn't see anything, but they heard a massive fall sound that they thought was a dropped haul-bag. I called Jano a few times but got no response. Then I heard John say, "Let him down!" I called Jano again, and then heard, "Let him down right now! Slow!" I did so until I heard, "Stop! Now call 911!"

[NPS—Jano had fallen about 65 feet. When they saw him suspended there, John and Anna soloed up a 45° slab formed by a huge flat chockstone leaning into the chimney while Stefan rappelled to them from the Spire. John and Stefan turned

Jano upright and tried to move him onto the slab, but Jano's leg had become wedged behind the slab and he was too heavy for them to lift.]

8:15 p.m: I tried to call but had no cell service. Then Anna yelled that she had fixed the static line Jano was trailing. I fixed the lead line to the belay anchor and ascended the static line as fast as possible.

8:22 p.m: I still couldn't see Jano, but John asked me to call 911 again and this time it worked. [Tibo had reached the Yosemite dispatcher.] I asked for a helicopter as soon as possible. I gave our location but couldn't answer the questions I was asked about the victim. [Tibo was needed up in the chimney immediately to help John and Stefan move Jano, so he hung up on the dispatcher.]

I needed to untie to reach the tiny ledge where Stefan and John [also untied] were holding Jano, in a half-seated position. I helped them move Jano two feet higher in order to be able to rotate his body [and release his leg]. At that point Jano's lead rope got tight [because I had tied it off earlier]. John asked Anna to cut it as low as possible, and while Stefan held the lead rope, we moved Jano to the bivy spot.

8:28 p.m: I called 911 once again to ask for a helicopter. They told me that it would be impossible because there was not enough light any more. When John heard this, he grabbed the phone and yelled that this is not a broken ankle issue but that the victim could die really soon and needed to be evacuated. He was told that there was really no way for the helicopter to fly at night. John understood, calmed down, and apologized. Like John, we all finally calmed down.

Jano was still seated, vomiting blood, and bleeding a lot from his skull. One eye was really swollen. We took off his helmet (which was broken in three places) and laid him down on his right side. All that time he was unconscious and unresponsive. He only mumbled a little, but at least he was still breathing. We placed him on two Thermarest pads and one sleeping bag and covered him with another sleeping bag (all John's and Anna's gear).

With one of my T-shirts I put pressure on what I thought was the wound on his head. Quickly the T-shirt became saturated with blood. I tried, unsuccessfully, to wash his head, and we then decided to put him on his other side. Jano finally showed signs of life and strongly resisted so we decided to leave him in the initial position.

Meanwhile it was getting cold and John went down to belay 19 to prepare our bag for hauling. The night was going to be cold and we were only wearing sweaters. Stefan went back up to the Spire and Anna started hauling our bag.

8:50 p.m: Anna, John, Jano, and I were all at the bivy spot in the Alcove. Anna tried to get some sleep in my sleeping bag. John stayed next to me under a thermal blanket we found in one of the first aid kits. All the bandages we found in the two kits did not last very long, and were quickly saturated. I had been next to Jano the whole time, trying to get his attention by talking to him all the time, but there was no response!

9 p.m.: I was getting scared that the bleeding was too much, and I tried to lift him up a little to check for a wound. There was a wound on the right side of his head, and I asked John for help to turn him onto his other side. It wasn't easy as Jano was firmly resisting, but still unconscious and with his eyes closed. Once on his left side, he finally stopped resisting and for the first time I could clearly see the size of the wound. I instantly made a compression point with my T-shirt.

[NPS—The Alcove team was trying to keep the blood and vomit draining out of Jano's mouth so it wouldn't choke him, but they were also worried about moving him at all, in case he had a broken neck, which it turned out later he did. When they removed Jano's helmet, they saw the blood pulsing out, as if from a scalp artery, and the signs of arterial bleeding coated the walls of the chimney where he had been hanging after the fall.]

10 p.m.: After one hour of seeing Jano unconscious, vomiting blood once again, I tried to release the compression point, afraid of hurting him more. But a thick flow was still leaking from his head. He had lost a lot of blood already and I returned the pressure to his wound. During this time John checked his ribs. I was worried that he had punctured his lungs because of all the blood he was spitting. John thought he could feel two broken ribs but his limbs seemed o.k.

May 21. 1 a.m.: John and I were really cold. We turned on a little gas stove but it was pretty much unsuccessful. Then John remembered he had noticed a backpack hidden [in the chimney]. We looked and found a heavy jacket and a North Face sleeping bag—lucky for us. We hesitated at first to use it, but we felt it was a real emergency and welcomed the warmth.

3:00 a.m: I had spent all night talking to Jano and maintaining the pressure point. I was totally exhausted and not really effective any more, so I woke John up and asked him to substitute for me. He took my place and fought his own fatigue.

4:30 a.m: I couldn't sleep and decided to give John a rest. I stayed next to Jano and talked to him continuously. I tried to get a response or a sign from him. We released the pressure point because the hemorrhage stopped. Once again we called 911. They asked us to measure his pulse and breathing rate. It was all good. John attempted to go back to sleep and I dozed off but set the alarm clock for 5:30 a.m. just in case.

5:30 a.m: The alarm clock rang, but I was already awake. The first light of the day brought along some hope.

6:00 a.m: Jano woke up. He didn't speak but tried to roll. We maintained his position firmly. His breathing was really shallow and was a lot less strong than earlier in the night. His hands and feet were getting cold.

6:30 a.m: Two helicopters arrived at El cap Meadow. One flew around us for reconnaissance.

7:00 a.m: A small [Calif. Highway Patrol] helicopter lowered a ranger-medic onto El Cap Spire. He rappelled to the Alcove and immediately attended to Jano, testing all his vitals. A few minutes later another flight brought another ranger-medic with four massive haul bags and a stretcher. Anna, John, and I helped strap Jano onto the stretcher.

8:00 a.m: The CHP helicopter returned and hoisted Jano from the ledge. It was a big relief for us to see him finally medically taken care of [after 11 hours].

Jano ended up with a skull fracture, a fractured C7, (fortunately it hasn't moved and won't generate any paralysis), and two broken ribs. The lungs were not punctured. It was the blood from inside his skull that Jano was spitting. Jano had surgery and should fully recover. After four days in a coma, he woke up and was able to eat and walk by himself.

I'd like to give a huge thanks to all those who participated in the rescue.

Analysis

Thibaut Mauron: Here are my conclusions about the accident: We all know the risks of the mountains and of climbing. We are aware of those, but accidents happen, and I have to confess I thought Jano wasn't going to make it through the night. But if I have one piece of advice, it is never give up and keep doing what's best for the victim.

NPS: As Tibo implies, this story is less about the accident itself than about the challenges you may face until the rescue agency arrives. It's rarely just like the classroom. The Alcove team was lucky in several respects: they had a bit of level terrain instead of hanging on the wall, they had enough daylight to get organized, they spoke a common language (English), they had cell service, and a capable rescue team was close by. But the most important ingredient was contributed by the climbers themselves—an aggressive and tenacious approach to the problem.

There was only one cell phone among the three parties, which could have been a problem, and no one had medical training beyond basic first aid. Nevertheless, they did an outstanding job with what they knew, and there wasn't much else they could have done in this case—get Jano off his rope, protect his airway and his neck, stop the bleeding, and hope for the best. (Source: Original article in French by Thibaut Mauron, translated to English by Laurent Cilia. Additional information from John and Anna. Edited for ANAM by John Dill and Jesse McGahey, NPS Rangers)

FALL ON ROCK, INADEQUATE BELAY ANCHOR/LOWERING ERROR – NYLON-ON-NYLON
California, Yosemite Valley, Royal Arches

On May 21, Curtis Rappe (24) climbed a single-pitch route near the base of Royal Arches while being belayed from below. At the top he threaded his rope directly through the nylon webbing slings of the anchor. As his partner lowered him, the friction of the rope melted through the slings and he fell about 20 feet to the ground.

Rangers responded to Rappe's 911 call. They found him complaining of pain to his hip, lower back, and chest. After carrying him to the road, they transferred him to an air ambulance that flew him to Doctors' Medical Center, Modesto. We don't have a final diagnosis, but he recovered fully.

Analysis

Rappe's prior climbing experience is unknown. It may have been minimal, since it is common knowledge that when nylon moves over nylon (or over any thermoplastic) with pressure between the two surfaces, the heat of friction building up on one spot can melt the fixed piece quickly. The rope must always be fed through a rappel ring, secure carabiner (locked or doubled), or other metal hardware designed for the purpose. (Source: John Dill, NPS Ranger)

(Editor's Note: We are continuing to see this kind of problem associated with rappelling and lowering. It's time for climbing stores and manufacturers of climbing ropes, slings, devices, and other paraphernalia to include some of the warnings that come out of these incidents.)

FALL ON ROCK, SELF-BELAY ERROR, MISTAKE WITH ASCENDERS, "SUMMIT FEVER"
California, Yosemite Valley, El Capitan

In late afternoon on June 3, Steve Gomez (37), Eric Sorenson (34), and Dave Goodwin (41), reached the last pitch of Mescalito (26 pitches, Grade VI) on El Capitan. Steve led the pitch but stopped briefly at the top of the bolt ladder, still on the steep headwall and four or five feet short of the final lip. To avoid rope drag, the guidebook advises hauling the bags to the top of the bolts first and then hauling the last few feet over the lip. Steve anchored the static haul line and the spare lead rope at the bolts and then climbed over the lip and 20 feet up the slab to the anchor tree at the top. Eric cleaned the whole pitch to the tree on Steve's lead rope while Dave jugged up to the bolts on the spare lead rope and hauled the bags that far. Here is what happened next, from Dave's perspective:

"I was left at the top of the bolt ladder to clean up the gear, release the bags for Steve and Eric to haul to the top, and get myself up. A section of Steve's lead line hung down to me from the tree and I was going to jug on that line. When I was ready to go, I looked down to check that I was tied in short to it just under my ascenders (Petzl Ascensions) in case I fell, and then I started to jug. It was about 6:30–7:00 p.m.

"After a few short steps up the headwall with my ascenders, I poked my head over the lip, where it turned into a low angle slab that you could just walk up. The lead rope was clipped through a quick draw at a fixed piton a foot or so over the lip. At the piton the rope turned about 45 degrees to the right and headed for the anchor tree, so my weight on the rope put the quick draw under tension, preventing me from unclipping from it. To pass the quick draw, I put all my weight on my lower (left-hand) ascender and then removed my upper (right-hand) ascender from the rope and reached up to reattach it above the piton. Both ascenders were connected to my harness by daisy chains, but for some reason my right daisy was much shorter than I normally rigged it; I was clipped to only the second or third loop from my harness, which restricted my reach, so I had to lean in to get as close to the wall as I could in order to place the ascender back on the rope. I thought I should stop trying to force the ascender into place and take time to lengthen the daisy, but the walk-off was literally two steps away and my hips were sore from the harness, so I thought, 'Forget it. I'll be finished in ten seconds.' So once I had reattached the ascender above the piton, I just hung onto it with my right hand for support and started bringing my right foot up above the lip, intending to make a high step and be done with the climb.

"I was halfway through the move, when the right ascender ripped off the rope. I don't remember the left one coming off but it obviously did, because I got shot out backward and started falling. I remember my left butt slamming into the wall part way down—a really intense impact—then falling some more, cart-wheeling, hitting again, and finally flipping upside down and coming to a stop. Later we estimated that I'd fallen 120–150 feet, and maybe more from rope stretch. As I was falling I'd had enough time to think, 'Why am I falling so far?' I thought I had tied in short so I figured my rope had been severed and I was going 2,500 feet to the deck.

"As I righted myself, Eric and then Steve poked their heads over the edge and yelled, 'Are you OK? What the #@%* happened?' 'Yeah, I'm not dead,' I replied, 'I believe I'm OK.' But I was in nervous shock and my left hip and left chest were extremely painful. Steve asked, 'Can you get yourself up or do we need to haul you? Can you move your arms and legs? Is your head OK?' I said, 'Steve, I have a serious shot of adrenaline and I think I have about ten minutes before my body shuts down, so I'm coming up!'

"I put my ascenders back on the rope, lengthened the right daisy this time, and started jugging. I would take ten steps, stop and breath, then ten more. I managed to keep it up for at least 30 minutes, tying in short frequently, until I was standing on top. On the way up I had been thinking, 'Oh my God, I gotta pass that pin, again,' but when I topped out I was surprised to find that the rope continued straight up to the anchor, bypassing the piton. It turned out that I had initially jugged on Steve's lead rope, as planned, but was only tied to the bottom end of the second lead rope. That rope, which I was now ascending, had caught me!"

[NPS comment: Eric had attached himself with a sling and a Grigri to what he thought was an unoccupied line and had come down to the edge to get the haul bags. As he was wrestling the bags up the slab, Dave was six feet to his left, starting to pass the piton. Eric wasn't looking at Dave at that moment but suddenly he heard a "snap" like a whip cracking and was surprised to see his own line go tight as it caught Dave's 150-footer! Eric decided it might be prudent to get off the rope they were sharing, so after initially calling down to Dave, he abandoned his Grigri—which was now jammed onto the line by Dave's weight—and jugged up to the anchor. Dave must have passed or removed the Grigri on his way up, though he may not remember it.]

"Eric helped me hobble along the hand line to safer ground, where Steve had prepared a place for me to lie down. Steve is a nurse, so he checked me over. I didn't think I'd shattered my hip because I'd jugged all that way on both legs, but Steve was worried that the pain under my rib cage might be a damaged spleen. He called 911 and explained everything to the rangers. There wasn't enough time to organize a helicopter rescue before dark and I seemed pretty stable, so they decided to wait. We stayed right there all night, with Steve having me pee in a cup periodically to check for blood. Early the next morning the NPS helicopter flew me to the park heli-base, where I was transferred to a med-evac helicopter for the flight to a hospital in Modesto. I got away with no broken bones and no spleen damage, but I had torn the muscles in my rib cage and severely bruised the bones in my hip. It took several months to recover and my lower back is still stiff, but I can get out and climb and ski again. I'm pretty lucky that the wall where I fell was so steep."

Analysis

"I didn't see what happened when my ascenders popped off, because I had shifted my gaze to my right foot placement. But I fell so far because I'd completely missed the fact that I had not tied in short. I've jugged many pitches over the years but this is the first time I've been so careless. It was probably a classic case of summit fever—on the wall seven days, only a few feet from topping out, and too much in a hurry to sort through the tangle of gear at the belay. When you check your tie in, identify the correct rope and run your fingers down it to the knot, make sure the carabiner is locked, and then double-check everything. I must have skipped all that and just looked down. And at that last piton I just kept going, intent on one last move, instead of fixing my daisy. You have to treat the whole climb like you do the first pitch, until you're all the way back down."

When an ascender is placed on the rope, it must be rotated into alignment parallel to the rope, or there is a risk that the angled rope will prevent the cam from closing completely, allowing the device to be accidentally torqued off the rope. This situation can easily occur on a traverse, so the 45° angle of Dave's rope and tension from his short daisy could have prevented proper alignment of his upper ascender after he thought he had reattached it to the rope. This possibility is not proven, but those pre-conditions have been found in a few previous ascender-related accidents in Yosemite, and we have been able to twist ascenders off the rope in simulated traverses in this manner. This is easily prevented by the user pushing the ascender parallel to the rope after attaching it and visually checking that the cam and safety catch have fully seated. Carabiners may also be clipped to the Petzl Ascension to keep the rope parallel. A second "failure" mechanism, of course, is when the user has simply forgotten to release the cam from the fully open position, and other mechanisms may exist.

We also do not know why the lower ascender came off. A web search for "ascender failure" leads to one claim of a Petzl releasing when the safety catch rubbed against the rock, but to properly relate this to Dave's case we would have to recreate the events, with Dave's rigging (and Dave), at the same location on Mescalito. Petzl's own instructions cover risks and proper use of their ascenders in illustrated detail and should be understood by every user.

We could fill another page in this article speculating about how Dave wound up on two different ropes and why he fell, but in the end, Dave has the best advice: "Tie in short, double-check everything, and recognize the symptoms of summit fever." (Source: Steve Gomez, Eric Sorenson, Dave Goodwin, and John Dill, NPS Ranger)

STRANDED ON DESCENT – UNABLE TO ASCEND ROPE, INADEQUATE SELF-RESCUE SKILLS, COMMUNICATIONS PROBLEMS OVER DISTANCE
California, Yosemite Valley, Sons of Yesterday

On June 29, Curt (26) and Sherri (29) (pseudonyms) climbed Serenity Crack (three pitches, 5.10d). From the top of Serenity they continued up Sons of Yesterday (six pitches, 5.10a), and then began rappelling the same line on double ropes. They reached the top of the first pitch of Sons (the bolts at the base of the long jam crack) in early afternoon and Curt descended first on the next rappel. As he neared the top of Serenity (the top of pitch 3), he saw that he had enough rope to reach the next anchor, so he called up to Sherri, told her his plan, and continued down to the top of pitch 2. Once there, he could not see or talk with Sherri, two pitches above, so he released tension on the rope and gave three tugs, their signal for her to rappel.

Curt discovered during his rappel that from their anchor on Sons the fall-line slanted distinctly left of his descent line, dropping over a steep corner onto the Superslide face to the west. Therefore, he had to deliberately tension to the right as he descended. He neglected to warn Sherri, assuming she would see the proper line and deal with it adequately. As she rappelled, Curt heard her start sliding along the rock and knew she was swinging left. She was barefoot, so once she lost her footing she couldn't regain it and she slid until she was hanging free, over the corner.

Curt still had the ends of the ropes, which ran up, left, and around the corner. He couldn't see what was on the other side, but Sherri was probably still 80 feet above and to his left. He tried pulling her toward him to where she could get herself around the corner and back onto the Serenity face, but there was too much friction. He decided to let go of the ends of the ropes. That left him marooned at the pitch 2 anchor, but it made it easier for Sherri to do whatever was necessary to get back up. At that point they could communicate somewhat by shouting, but Curt didn't realize that she was hanging free. Although the area is very popular, they saw no other climbers on Serenity or Superslide to help them.

To get out of their jam, Sherri would have to ascend her ropes until she was above the lip and high enough on the face that she could swing back onto the correct line. (It would also help if she put her shoes back on for friction.) She had slings with which to fashion Prusiks or other ascender hitches, but she didn't know how to tie them and had never ascended a rope that way. Curt tried to talk her through it but failed because of the poor communication conditions.

Sherri continued her rappel onto the Superslide face. Now she could see and talk with Curt but there was no way to link up, so she found natural anchors, continued to the ground, and called the Park Service. Two rescuers climbed Serenity Crack so Curt could descend.

Analysis

The route topo, which Curt and Sherri had taken up the climb, warns about the risk of swinging left on that rappel. If you spot such a hazard, as Curt did, don't assume your partner will see it. If the issue is significant, point it out and keep the rappels short for better communications. But stuff happens despite your best efforts, so it pays to have the skills to get yourself out of trouble. Re-ascending the rope as soon as she took the slider would have put Sherri back on track (with a bit of sweat), but despite six years of experience and leading multi-pitch trad at the 5.9–5.10 level, she did not know how to safely ascend a rope. Overall, this was a pretty minor incident, but a slight change of scene—instead of only 300 yards from Yosemite Village—might have left them both stranded.

[Technical Note: I hate to see climbing come to this, but if they'd both had cell phones and service, Curt could have sent instructional photos to Sherri on the spot. A pair of FRS radios is the next best solution, but having self-rescue skills beats both options.] (Source: John Dill, NPS Ranger, and Curt)

FALL ON ROCK, FREE-SOLOING
California, Yosemite – Tuolumne Meadows, Cathedral Peak

On the afternoon of July 9th, rangers received a report that a climber had fallen approximately 400 to 500 feet while descending the Eichorn Pinnacle on Cathedral Peak. Rangers responded by helicopter and quickly located the climber, identified as Christina Chan (31). Her body was removed from the scene via short-haul by a park contract helicopter.

Analysis

Chan was a very experienced climber, with roped-solo ascents of difficult Grade VI routes on El Capitan. According to those who interacted with her on Cathedral Peak that day, she was in good spirits and climbing with skill and confidence. Eric Cohen caught a glimpse of about 20 feet of Chan's fall, but no one knows what caused it. Free-soloing is here to stay, but even the lowest grade levels can be fatal when the rope is left in the car. (Source: John Dill and Jesse McGahey, NPS Rangers)

FALL ON ROCK – BELAY FAILURE (UNSECURED ROPE, DISTRACTION), NO HELMET
California, Yosemite Valley, Five Open Books

On August 11, my brothers, Eric (26) and Thayne (19), and I, Grace Rich (31), were visiting Yosemite and we decided to go climbing. Eric and Thayne had climbed only a few times before and weren't feeling up for a multi-pitch route, so I thought we'd just do the first pitch of Munginella (three pitches, 5.6), a route I'd climbed before.

From the base of the wall we had to scramble 50 feet up to the belay ledge at the start of the pitch. I led the pitch, set the anchors at the top, and had Thayne start lowering me with his belay device. My parents had come up to watch and everyone was chatting, so Thayne was distracted. The rope was piled in front of him, but he was looking up at me when Eric noticed just a second too late that the rope was too short. The end of the rope went through the belay device because I hadn't tied a knot in it.

My first thought, when there was no tension on the rope, was "Funny, Thayne!" I thought he was letting a little bit of rope go just to scare me, but then it never caught and I realized I was falling, 30 feet above the belay ledge and 80 feet above the ground. I think I hit my heels on a little lip on the face and it flipped me upside down; I hit my whole lower back and butt area pretty hard. My brothers knew that if they didn't stop me at the belay ledge, I would keep going another 50 feet. Luckily they tackled me and Eric may have saved my life by getting under me and cushioning my fall, but I hit my head on a sharp rock when I landed and ripped my scalp open. My dad ran down to get help and we put pressure on my scalp to stop the bleeding while I tried to get my bearings.

To my embarrassment, the search and rescue team came up. I kept trying to feel OK about getting down myself. I never blacked out so I thought I was pretty well off, but both my ankles were swelling and my pelvis hurt, so I swallowed my pride and decided to do what Matt—the ranger in charge—

suggested, and let them immobilize me in a litter, lower me to the ground, and carry me down the hill.

An ambulance transferred me to a med-evac helicopter that flew me to a hospital in Modesto. I tried to fight that as well, but Matt explained that I needed X-rays or CTs to check for fractures and that I should have an experienced ER staff clean and sew up the huge six-inch flap on my scalp.

In Modesto, they could find no broken bones. They sutured my scalp and released me, but a follow-up CT six weeks later back home showed that I had five fractures in the talus bone in my left ankle. I'm now recovering from surgery and carrying hardware in my foot, but I should eventually be back in action.

Analysis

A lot of dumb factors went into this accident and I don't blame Thayne. I've been climbing frequently for 16 years and lead 5.9–5.10, so you'd think I'd know better by now. The responsibility was all mine. I should have worn my helmet, tied a knot in the end of the rope, and told Thayne to look for the half way mark on the rope.

I'd unintentionally left my helmet behind, but admittedly I wasn't good about wearing one anyway—and the route was easy. I had previously climbed the entire route, so rope length wasn't an issue then, and this time I didn't even think about the rope being too short. I had also been lazy about tying knots in the end. No one I climb with really does that and it just never crossed my mind. The new Grace will pay more attention from now on.

NPS comments: A few injures of this kind happen every year in Yosemite (at least the ones we hear about), and they are not restricted to inexperienced belayers. See examples in ANAM 2009 and 2008. The fact that the climbers survived may be due to the relatively short falls when the rope runs out, but a fatality will eventually occur. Grace was extremely lucky that she didn't receive a more serious head injury and she has her brothers to thank for keeping her from going the rest of the way. (Source: John Dill, NPS Ranger, and Grace Rich)

FALLING ROCK – BLOCK CAME OFF, FALL ON ROCK – INADEQUATE PROTECTION, BAD LUCK/GOOD LUCK
California, Yosemite Valley, El Capitan

On August 24 in late afternoon, Kyung Bok Su (47) and three Korean partners finished pitch 19 of the Nose route (31 pitches, Grade VI) and Kyung began leading pitch 20 up to Camp IV. He climbed up and left to a large block, placed a cam near its base, then climbed up his aid ladder and made one or two layback moves with his hands in the crack on the right side of the block. Suddenly a large piece of the block broke off and Kyung fell with it.

The cam failed and he either had no other protection in place below him or it all failed, because Kyung swung to the right and slammed into the wall about 35 feet below the belay. This impact probably caused his injury, later diagnosed as a broken left femur (in two places).

As he hung there, he noticed that over two feet of the sheath of his lead rope was stripped from the core just in front of his harness and a few core strands were severed. (The cause is unknown but probably the falling rock.) One of the team's other ropes happened to be hanging within reach, so he attached his ascenders to it and his partners managed to pull him up to the belay.

The party called on their FRS radio, "Rescue, El Capitan!" They heard other traffic but no one responded to their transmissions. They also yelled and waved jackets and finally someone in El Cap Meadow noticed them and contacted the NPS. The park helicopter, H551, was able to place a team on the summit just before dark to begin rigging for rescue. Meanwhile a ranger in the meadow communicated with Kyung's party by telescope and loudspeaker. He learned that Kyung had not lost consciousness, had no difficulty breathing and no head/neck pain, and was moving his limbs purposefully, so the summit team decided to minimize risk by delaying the operation until daylight. The next morning, additional rescuers joined them, and two medics were lowered about 1000 feet to the scene. They packaged Kyung in a litter and short-hauled him directly from the ledge with H551. He was transferred to an air ambulance and flown to Memorial Medical Center in Modesto.

Analysis

Kyung's partners did not see exactly what happened and we're not sure how he protected the pitch, although he may have placed only the single cam. His fall is a good example of the risks of swinging sideways—and thereby striking the really critical parts of your body. For more on swinging falls, see Tony Alegre's accident—following this one—and keep this risk in mind when protecting.

One of the rescue rangers said both ends of rope were poorly anchored and the climbers did not back themselves up to the bolt anchor. They said the anchors were cams and that the rope was clipped to the bolts. A photo shows a sling clipped around the rope but not into it. (Source: John Dill, NPS Ranger)

FALL ON ROCK – MISJUDGED PENDULUM
California, Yosemite Valley, El Capitan

On Sept. 18, Toni Alegre (42) and Jorge Lantero (43) started climbing the Nose of El Capitan (31 pitches, Grade VI). They led on double ropes (one red and one green) and moved quickly, practicing for a later attempt to climb the route in a day. From the anchor at the top of pitch 6, Lantero pendulumed into the left-facing corner about 30 feet to the right and began climbing the corner. As he placed protection, he clipped only his red rope through the pieces, but after several placements he began clipping both ropes. Using this method he protected all of pitch 7 for himself while also leaving a high pivot point for the green rope, so that when Alegre followed him on green, he would swing slowly across without risk of injury.

When Lantero reached the pitch 7 anchor and looked down, however, he realized that he might have clipped the green rope too low on the pitch. He warned Alegre that he might swing too fast into the corner because of the large pendulum angle. Alegre had looked at the corner and decided he could jump over it if necessary, so he replied that the move appeared to be safe and asked Lantero to pull up the excess rope. He let himself out partway with a sling in order to reduce the angle and then he let go. As he swung over, he found that a bulge in the wall had hidden the corner's actual size. He was unable to leap over it and struck it sideways harder than expected.

Alegre knew right away that his right femur was broken. (He was lucky that it was a "closed" fracture, i.e., there was no open wound.) He called 911 with his cell phone while Lantero rappelled to assist him. With no ledge nearby to rest on, they hung from the ends of their ropes for two hours waiting for rescue.

The NPS helicopter was able to insert two rescuers directly to the scene by short-haul. They stabilized Alegre's injuries and short-hauled him off the cliff to a med-evac helicopter waiting in El Capitan Meadow. He reached the hospital in Modesto about four hours after the accident. It turned out he had also cracked two ribs and his right forearm, but he expects to make a full recovery.

Analysis

In hindsight, Alegre and Lantero agree that Alegre should have lowered himself across the gap with the unused portion of the green rope. There was plenty of rope to do so, but even with a short rope, getting halfway can sometimes be enough to safely complete the swing.

Underestimating pendulums is a fairly common cause of serious injuries and it often involves experienced climbers. (Alegre and Lantero are climbing guides. For another recent example, see Ruderman, El Capitan, ANAM 2009.)

Why are pendulums so dangerous? First, the kinetic energy you develop swinging from your high point to your low point is the same as if you had fallen straight down the same vertical distance. It's simply redirected sideways by the rope. Second, if you strike a corner, the impact will likely be to your head, trunk, pelvis—all potentially life-threatening. You may be able to extend (and sacrifice) an arm or a leg to absorb the blow, but you also may be tumbling out of control. Third, it's easy to underestimate the risk, because a dihedral 15 feet to the side just doesn't look as dangerous as a ledge 15 feet below you. So before you cut loose, estimate your total vertical drop, and if you might hit an obstacle, ask yourself if you would like to fall that distance straight down onto concrete and land on your side. (You face a similar risk if a leader fall will send you swinging into the wall. See Kyung, El Capitan, Previous report in this issue.) (Source: Toni Alegre, Jorge Lantero, and John Dill, NPS Ranger)

FALL ON ROCK – FAILURE TO BELAY THUMB
California, Yosemite Valley, El Capitan

On Oct 12, Matt Krueger (41) and I, John Robinson (64), started climbing up to Sickle Ledge from the base of El Cap, intending to fix our lines for a head start on the Nose route the following day. We third-classed up the buttress, Matt led the first pitch, and I began leading the second. Halfway up I made the pendulum to the next crack on the right. I immediately clipped through a fixed pin and then I continued up on aid, setting two pieces above the pin. I knew that my top piece wasn't very good, but it was the best I could find. I was high-stepping above it in my etrier, trying to put in something higher, when it pulled. For some reason I had neglected to clip through the previous piece—just above the pin, so I fell about 30 feet and was caught by the fixed pin and the bolts from which I had made the pendulum.

As I started to fall, I felt a severe pain in my left thumb. When I stopped falling, I saw just a stump above the distal knuckle, with blood gushing out. Then I looked down to see the end of my thumb falling 400 feet to the bottom of the cliff. I was sure we wouldn't be able to find it, as it went into bushes and rocks. I clamped my other hand over my thumb to stop the bleeding. Matt lowered me until I was even with him, threw a rope over to me, and pulled me to the belay. He then lowered me to a tree that we could rappel from. Our friend Curt was hanging out at the base. He called the Park Service, then he free-climbed up Pine Line (one pitch, 5.7) using his ATC and a fixed rope for a belay, transferred me to another rope, and lowered me the rest of the way. An ER doctor happened to be hiking by at the base of the cliff. He looked at my thumb and said, "Oh man, I don't think they can reattach that." A ranger came up, wrapped the stump, and walked me out to a waiting ambulance.

Meanwhile Curt and Matt started looking for the tip of my thumb. I told them that they would never find it because of the broken and bushy terrain and the wide area into which it could have fallen. Fortunately they didn't listen to me. Curt got other climbers to assist; they scaled ledges and crawled through the bushes and one of them found it just before dark. The ranger wrapped it in sterile gauze moistened with saline and Curt gave him the ice pack from his lunch box to keep it cool. By this time I was well on my way out of the park in the ambulance. The ranger radioed us and said he was driving with the thumb, Code 3, to catch us. In El Portal we met another ambulance that would take me to a med-evac helicopter at Mariposa. (It was too dark for the helicopter to land at Yosemite, and the initial ambulance needed to stay in the park.) My thumb also met us at the rendezvous.

The second ambulance crew made a number of calls and were told that we (my thumb and I) should be flown to Fresno where the reattachment could be attempted. But when we reached the hospital, the doctor there said they didn't do reattachments. Somehow the communications had been garbled and, needless to say, I wasn't very happy. They tried to make up for it by fast-tracking all the necessary x-rays, blood/urine tests, ECG, and other preliminaries for surgery while waiting for another helicopter to arrive. Eventually we reached San Francisco International Airport. (We couldn't land at the hospital because San Francisco is a noise-free zone, according to my flight nurse.) Another ambulance took me to the California Pacific Medical Center in San Francisco, where they specialize in reattachment surgery.

The fall occurred at about 1745 and now it was midnight. I was concerned that too much time had elapsed for reattachment, but the surgeons said if no muscle is involved, the time frame isn't as critical; however, reattachment still might not be possible. After surgery, if my thumb was wrapped completely, it was not successful. If the end was exposed with two pins sticking out, it was successful. When I awoke, I saw two pins, so I was happy. Recovery included five days confined to bed—no exceptions—while leeches drained excess blood from my thumb. The pins came out after five weeks, then I had more weeks of physical therapy, and I'm now back to climbing. The thumb still lacks some feeling and strength, but it turns out I don't need it for most moves.

Analysis

There are lots of warning about keeping your digits away from the eyes of pitons and the cables of camming devices, but I can't "finger" a culprit in this case. I remember that the pain occurred at the beginning of the fall, not the end. I was high-stepping and my left hand was holding on to something near the top of the étriér—probably my daisy or the little grab loop on the etrier, but not the cam itself, I think—while I reached high with my right hand to set the next piece. The surgeons said the tip of the thumb was pulled off, not cut off, and it's hard to see what could have grabbed it so tightly. I've thought about it a lot, but I still don't know what happened. (Source: John Robinson, Curt Taras, and John Dill, NPS Ranger)

FALL ON ROCK – BELAY FAILURE (UNSECURED ROPE, DISTRACTION)
California, Yosemite Valley, Churchbowl

On Nov. 6, Betsey (20) and I, Mike (19), (pseudonyms) spent the day climbing at Churchbowl with friends. I had climbed in the park several times over the last three years, but that was my first time at Churchbowl. I led several climbs and rigged top ropes for the others to follow, using a 60-meter rope.

About 1600, I went over to do Churchbowl Lieback (one pitch, 5.8). It was an hour or so before dark and I was trying to squeeze in some more routes. I unflaked the rope quickly, and then I called everyone over, without thinking about whether I had tied a knot at the bottom end of the rope. Another group of climbers came over to watch and to wait for their turn.

I led the pitch while Betsey belayed me from the ground. At the top I backed up the slings on the anchor tree, added 'biners for the top rope, and asked Betsey to lower me.

There is a ledge about ten feet above the ground, and when I was about three feet above it, the rope started feeding out faster and I began slipping. I didn't know what was happening and I yelled to Betsey to stop me, but the end of the rope had run through her belay device, so of course she couldn't stop me. I noticed rocks on the ground directly below and I may have pushed myself backwards off the wall in the right direction, because somehow I managed to land in the dirt next to the rocks. I hit hard on my butt and then my back, and rolled down the hill. The wind was knocked out of me and I couldn't even say "I'm OK."

A friend climbing nearby heard me hit and immediately came over, stabilized my neck, and had me lie on my back. My whole lower back hurt on both sides. Someone called 911 and the ambulance (which was at the clinic only a couple of hundred yards away) was there in minutes. At the clinic the staff checked me over head-to-toe and decided nothing was broken, so they let me go. I had minor sprains and a tiny bit of blood in my urine suggestive of a mild kidney contusion, but everything felt fine within a week. I was lucky to miss the rocks.

Analysis

Mike: I had read about the route in the past but had forgotten that our guidebook advised belaying from the ledge, not the ground. When I walked over to the route I did not even think about rope length. I'd never been on a climb where the rope was this short, and I think the reason I got used to not always tying knots is from the gym, where you are sure the rope is long enough. Also, most of my trad climbing is multi-pitch, so the second is always tied in. From now on I'll knot the end or leave it tied to the rope bag. My rope will also have a mid-mark. Finally, I normally do not wear a helmet on short climbs, but I will never not (sic) wear one again.

Betsey: I think a flaw in our climbing relationship is that Mike is more experienced and generally the leader, so he is always the one who initially checks the rigging. He'll say, "OK, we're ready to go," and I'll do a quick double-check, as he's trained me to do, and we go. We often tie a knot in the end of the rope, but this time I wasn't thinking as thoroughly and independently as I should have been, so I didn't double-check. During the climb the rope was in view, piled on the bag to my right as I faced the wall.

I'm a competent belayer, but I was looking up at Mike and chatting with the other climbers, who were to my left and a little behind me. I became distracted long enough to forget about the end of the rope. (Source: Betsey, Mike, and John Dill, NPS Ranger)

(Editor's Note: There were many more incidents in Yosemite than appear here. The good news is that there were no serious bouldering mishaps. The bad news is that there was a total of 19 leader fall accidents, 11 cases involving rappelling, belay errors, rockfall, etc. A serious rockfall—200-pound block—struck one climber on Tangerine trip in December, resulting in a two-day rescue operation. Not all of them made it into Table III because not enough details were available. Special thanks to John Dill and Jesse McGahey, Yosemite rangers, for their assiduous work in compiling and following up on incidents, including interviewing climbers involved.)

FALL ON ICE, ICE PILLAR FRACTURED
Colorado, Vail, The Fang

On January 12, MM (34) and KS partnered up to climb a 35-meter pillar of ice known as The Fang (WI5). MM instructed KS on their approach where to stand for a safe belay. MM started his lead by climbing on the opposite side of the cauliflower to the base of the pillar where he set a screw and moved to the west side of the pillar. Setting another screw, MM moved back around and back cleaned his first placement. He regained the start of his line, and continued confidently up the pillar, making a few light-hearted comments about his protection and obviously having fun. MM placed approximately six screws in the pillar. He was above his last screw by about five meters and approximately 30 meters from the ground, and after placing his feet and setting his right tool, the next swing with the left, the pillar seemingly imploded below him.

The climber's hands, as reported by a close witness, were above the fracture line and the ice seemed to fall a fraction of a second before the climber. Clouded by a plume of ice dust the rest of the fall was not witnessed. He came to rest on the viewer's right, about three meters from the formation. KS reached MM within seconds and began his rapid assessment. Multiple climbers in the area began a rapid and efficient evacuation. MM was loaded into a ski area litter and lowered two 60-meter pitches of low angle snow and ice, where paramedics were met and informed of the patient's issues. It took two hours or less in total and MM arrived at Vail Valley Medical Center.

Analysis

A number of positive influences and emotions set up for a bad decision to climb The Fang on this day. A few other local friends who are experienced climbers in the area showed nothing but positive views and support for MM's interest of climbing the formation that day. Very few negative concerns were expressed. MM had been in the area consistently since early

December on essentially a full time basis. While the formation grew, he had closely been studying the conditions of the pillar. The pillar had seen two previous ascents. One ascent that MM was aware of was made by a local friend of the area. The climber had previously talked to MM about his ascent. Conditions seemed good for MM that day. He was mentally and physically prepared for the climb. The technical climbing wouldn't be the issue. Knowledge, experience and acceptable risk all played a major role in this incident. (Source: Marc Boilard, member of party and rescuer)

FALL ON ICE, BELAY DEVICE SET-UP INCORRECTLY
Colorado, Ouray Ice Park

According to reports, on February 6, a client topped out and placed his partner, a guide, on belay. In the process, the client rigged his Reverso incorrectly. Sometime during the climb the climber was being lowered and because the rope was threaded incorrectly through the belay device, the guide was dropped 40 feet, resulting in a broken pelvis along with a few other bones.

Analysis

A good practice to follow before going on belay is to do a pull test on all autoblock devices when they are in autoblock mode, even if you're sure the device is threaded the right way. (Source: www.mountainproject.com)

STRANDED, OFF ROUTE
Colorado, Eldorado Canyon State Park

On March 4, a male climber (23) and his friend began to rappel the Redguard route sometime around 7:00 p.m. They quickly realized they had descended in the wrong spot and had become stuck. They called two friends who attempted to help them, but after several hours they decided to call 911. Rocky Mountain Rescue performed a technical rescue of the two stuck climbers, and evacuated them without incident and injury.

Analysis

A better knowledge of the descent route may have prevented this incident from occurring. (Source: Boulder County Sheriff's Department)

FALL ON ROCK, NO HARD HAT
Colorado, Boulder Falls

During the afternoon on March 6, a person reported a fallen climber in the area behind Boulder Falls by flagging down a United States Forest Service employee, who in turn reported the incident by radio.

The climber, Austin Forbes (21), was located at the base of the Plotinus Wall, a popular sport climbing area. He had fallen approximately 20 feet while lead climbing, suffering a skull fracture, lung contusion, and left shoulder dislocation. Forbes had been climbing with William Hausen (19) and another individual. Forbes was not wearing a helmet. Forbes was treated by paramedics and then evacuated to the road by the Rocky Mountain Rescue Group. *[NB: The climbing party accessed the Plotinus Wall through the Boulder Falls area, which is currently closed by the City of Boulder due to rock-fall hazard. City of Boulder Rangers cited Hausen for trespassing in the closed area.]* (Source: http://cuindependent.com)

AVALANCHE, CLIMBING ALONE
Colorado, Cimmaron Mountains, Baldy Peak

On March 30, Heidi Kloos (41), traveling with her dog, went to climb a remote ice climb on the northeast side of Baldy Peak (10,603 feet). Ouray County Search and Rescue was contacted on March 31 when a friend found that Heidi had not returned home.

A small team went to assess the scene and discovered the avalanche. Ouray County Search and Rescue found tracks leading into a large avalanche debris pile. Heidi had left her pack and climbing gear, including an avalanche beacon, just outside of the avalanche debris. The assumption was that Heidi dropped her gear and headed up to assess the climb and was caught low in the path. Her dog was also found at the scene.

Darkness hampered further rescue efforts until the next day. A larger rescue team and two avalanche rescue dogs and their handlers arrived at the staging area early on the morning of April 1. A team of two went into the area, followed shortly thereafter by the dog teams. After several hours of searching the complex terrain, a dog team located a ski. The ski was found at the toe of the debris, in line with the clues that were found the day before (pack, climbing skin). Rescuers decided to do a probe search up the likely line of trajectory. After about 45 minutes, rescuers felt they had a strike and dug down to confirm. One of the avalanche dogs also gave an alert in this area. Rescuers continued to dig and found Heidi buried under five to six feet snow and debris.

Heidi had 15 years of experience guiding big mountains around the world. She was a very experienced backcountry traveler and a certified alpine mountain guide (AMGA). She had completed professional level avalanche safety training (AIARE Level III).
Analysis
It is ill advised to travel alone in avalanche country. (Source: Colorado Avalanche Information Center)

FALL ON ROCK, PROTECTION PULLED OUT
Colorado, Boulder Canyon, Happy Hour Crag

On May 8, I took a 15-foot ground fall at Happy Hour, resulting in three broken ribs and a partially collapsed lung. Very lucky! I was leading "I, Robot" (5.7), a right-facing dihedral. There's not a lot of gear off the ground. I had a 0.5 cam in the crack about ten feet up and I had backed it up with a small stopper above it. I was trying to get above the gear and took a short fall. The gear held. I didn't re-set the gear or even look at it after that fall, because I figured the stopper would be well sunk into the rock at that point. Mistake? I just don't know.

I tried again, and managed to get my feet several feet above the gear and was on a small ledge. The crack wasn't great, so neither the holds nor the places for gear were very great. I found a spot on the left side where I could have jammed a cam in there, but I didn't have enough time.

I peeled off. I was off balance, so I swung out to the right and then down. I remember seeing my gear. At that point, I had no idea it wouldn't hold. I didn't even know I was going to deck until I was already down.

Analysis

I've tried to analyze my gear placement with friends and I have two thoughts about it. I should have at least checked the placement after my first fall. But it's possible that the reason it popped was the angle of the fall. (Source: Kitty Turner from a post on mountainproject.com)

PRE-EXISTING CONDITION
Colorado, Boulder Canyon

On May 29, Bill Trull (age unknown) was climbing in a recently developed climbing area across from the Bihedral Rock. The climb was located on the south side of Boulder Creek. Trull did not fall but became injured during the climb due to a previous, unrelated injury. He was climbing on a top rope and was lowered to the base of the climb.

When the Boulder Fire ladder truck arrived it was determined the ladder would reach across the river at a narrow point. The ladder was extended across the river and Trull was loaded into the ladder bucket and brought back across the river.

Analysis

Climbers with pre-existing medical conditions should be checked by a personal physician before climbing. Pre-existing conditions can compromise the outcome of a rock climb for both the climber and climbing party by creating unanticipated problems. (Source: www.bouldercounty.org)

FALL ON ROCK, POOR POSITION
Colorado, Eldorado Canyon, Redgarden Wall

On June 15, Emily Cosnett (29) was climbing with Eric Dunlap on the The Yellow Spur (5.9). Emily was positioned on the ground and had Eric on-belay. Eric slipped about eight feet up the climb and fell, landing on Emily. Emily suffered a laceration to her left eye, and complained of back and neck pain and numbness in her left leg. Medical care was provided on scene by rescuers and Emily was evacuated out of the field. Emily was wearing a climbing helmet.

Analysis

Belayers should make an effort to position themselves out of the fall line of the climber. (Source: Boulder County Sheriff's Office and Steve Muehlhauser, Park Ranger, Eldorado Canyon State Park)

CLIMBER PULLED ROCK OFF, ROCK FALL
Colorado, Eldorado Canyon, Wind Tower

On June 17 rescuers were called to Eldorado Canyon State Park for a rockslide with a person trapped. Selma Hafizbegovic (39) was going to climb the Wind Tower rock formation via the Recon Route (5.6). She was with four other climbers, all from New York. Selma was walking near the group when two of her friends began to climb. When the first climber started up, he pulled down a large rock they described as being approximately the size of a person. Selma, who was standing below, was swept down a ravine approximately fifty feet with the rocks. She was not trapped in the rubble. They were all wearing helmets.

She was evacuated by members of the Rocky Mountain Rescue Group and Rocky Mountain Fire and flown to a Denver area hospital. Her injuries resulted in paralysis. (Source: From a Boulder County Sheriff's Department press release and http://www.eventme.com)

FALL ON ROCK, SIMUL-CLIMBING
Colorado, Eldorado Canyon State Park

On June 26, Bill Wright (45) and Tom Karpeichik (48) attempted to simul-climb 100 pitches in Eldorado Canyon (Eldo) in a day. At about 7:30 a.m. the climbers were on their 11th route/34th pitch on Redguard Route (5.8) when the higher climber fell about 140 feet and sustained serious injuries. Fortunately the few points of protection between the climbers held. A trail runner in the park heard calls for help and initiated a rescue. Both climbers were wearing helmets. The victim's helmet likely saved his life.

Analysis

In contrast to the traditional stationary belayer and one active climber at-a-time technique, simul-climbing sacrifices safety for speed and has both climbers climbing at the same time with only a few points of protection between them at any given time. This technique alone wasn't the reason this fall was so traumatic. It is highly likely that if he were leading this pitch in a traditional manner, he would have placed more gear, since he would only be climbing for 150 feet or so.

His partner said, "…if we had been climbing in a traditional manner and using a standard-length rope, I would have been able to escape the belay and rappel to Tom on the unused portion of the rope. What caused Tom to fall on 5.5/5.6 terrain? I don't know. Maybe Tom doesn't either or will not remember, but a slip is the most probably answer. I didn't see any rock fall with him and it is unlikely that a hold broke." (Source: Steve Muehlhauser, Park Ranger, Eldorado Canyon State Park, and Bill Wright, from a post on www.mountainproject.com)

FALL ON ROCK, ROPE SEVERED
Colorado, Eldorado Canyon State Park, Red Garden Wall

Joe Miller (38) fell to his death on the morning of June 22 while climbing the Yellow Spur route (5.9) on the Redgarden Wall. A later investigation revealed that a micro-Camalot below the dihedral held. It appears that the length of sling on that cam caused the rope to run over a particularly sharp edge, severing the fairly new 60-meter, 9.8-mm rope resulting in a fall of seventy feet to the ground for Miller.

Analysis

An investigation by the Rocky Mountain Rescue Group found no problem with the rope, but did look into the angles of the rope, etc. See their full analysis at http://www.rockymountainrescue.org. Lead climbers are encouraged to inspect the immediate area before placing gear. Check for sharp edges, loose rock, expanding flakes, etc., and react accordingly. (Source: Jed Williamson and Steve Muehlhauser, Park Ranger, Eldorado Canyon State Park)

RAPPEL ERROR – NO BACK-UP BELAY AND NO KNOT ON ROPE END
Colorado, Boulder Canyon

On July 6, a female (31) fell approximately 15 feet when she rappelled off the end of her rope while climbing in Boulder Canyon. She injured her lower leg, and possibly her back, and had to be transported across Boulder Creek and taken to Boulder Community Hospital.

Analysis

It is common practice to tie a blocking knot on the free end of the rope as a rappel safeguard. (Source: www.dailycamera.com/news)

FALL ON ROCK
Colorado, Rocky Mountain National Park, Longs Peak

On July 17, my partner Eric Baer (23) and I (William Esposito, 27) began climbing the Stettner's Ledges Route (5.7+) on the east face of Longs Peak. On approximately the fourth pitch, I climbed about ten feet past my last gear placement, a green Camalot, and as I attempted a technical climbing maneuver I lost my grip on the rock and fell. I shouted, "Falling," and fell past my cam placement about ten feet. The Camalot held and the rope caught me, but the approximately two feet of rope stretch caused both of my feet to smash onto a ledge of rock. I quickly shouted down to Eric that I was OK; however, after about thirty seconds of rest, I realized both of my feet had been severely damaged (small fracture in talus bone of left foot, severe soft tissue damage in both).

Eric carefully lowered me to the belay ledge he was on. From there, he used existing anchors as well as our own equipment to lower me first, then himself back down three pitches to the Mills Glacier. He then used the rope to control my slide down the glacier to a flat rock. Eric made sure I had adequate food, water, and clothing and then went for help.

Eric returned about an hour later with another climber with first re-sponder training who had sent his partner down for help. Two additional climbing parties of two each came down from climbing routes on the Diamond. One of them had a cell phone that worked and called for rescue. About an hour later, two climbing rescue rangers arrived. One arranged for a helicopter while the other performed a medical examination on me. I was then laid into a stretcher and carried by the rangers and other climbers (eight people) 200 yards across snow and rock to the helicopter landing spot. The helicopter arrived approximately one hour from the time the rangers arrived. I was taken to the Boulder Community Hospital, treated for my injuries and the released the same evening.

Analysis

Although everything worked just as it should, I should have been more aware of my fall line at all times. Because I climbed ten feet past my last gear placement, I should have considered the ledge ten feet below it and perhaps placed more gear before continuing. This incident reinforces the importance of having the skills and knowledge to initiate self-rescue. (Source: William Esposito)

FALL ON ROCK, ROCK and MUD SLIDES
Colorado, Crestone Needle

Duane (57) and Linda Buhrmester (56), both experienced climbers, walked in from the trailhead to Upper Colony Lake on July 26 in the mid afternoon. They camped there for the night with the intent on climbing the Ellingwood Arête (5.7+) on Crestone Needle (14,197 feet).

Investigators suggested that a severe storm washed the couple off the mountain, causing them to fall about 500 feet into a mudslide area. Rescuers found the couple buried in rocks and mud. We believe this is what happened because they weren't roped together when found (Linda had a mountaineer's coil over her shoulder and had both ends of the rope, suggesting they had used the rope earlier and had it at the ready should they need it again). If they were in that chute with that much scree, they knew that it would have been safest for them to not be tied together because of the potential for the rope to get caught on loose rock and cause rockfall.

Analysis

Family members speculate that the couple would have gotten up well before dawn, knowing that weather could be an issue. Family members found only one eaten dinner in the couple's tent and several more days worth of food, suggesting they attempted the summit on July 27.

They likely saw the weather was changing for the worse at some point on the Ellingwood Arête route—unsure when, but it's fairly certain they did not summit because they would have descended the standard route. But that's not where they were found. They had also not eaten their packed lunch, which they would normally do on the summit. Upon seeing the weather changing, they would have tried to descend as safely and quickly as possible. It's likely they rappelled or down-climbed to the gully/chute adjacent to the route where it probably looked as the safest and most direct route down to camp.

Both climbers were found wearing their boots and had their rock shoes in their packs, suggesting that they had not taken a fall on a technical pitch where they would have been wearing their rock shoes. Family members suspect they got pretty high up the arête in their rock shoes, bailed, and switched to boots, as they probably didn't want to twist an ankle in their rock shoes on any loose scree, then encountered a rock slide. Based on where they were found and the likely weather issues, we think this is what happened. The bodies were found four days after the storm.

During and after rain, climbers should expect to encounter slippery rock and terrain in general and adjust their movement accordingly. In heavy rain, expect flash floods or debris slides in gullies or chimneys. In some cases climbers can be washed away or drowned if caught in a large gully during a rainstorm and be aware of falling rock that may have been loosened by running water. (Source: Michael Buhrmester, www.14er.com)

STRANDED, OFF ROUTE, PARTY SEPARATED
Colorado, Rocky Mountain National Park, Longs Peak, The Diamond

On July 20, Carloyn Davis (27) became stranded while rappelling down The Diamond (East Face). She and her partner had climbed the Casual Route (grade IV, 5.10) and reached Table Ledge where the Diamond rappels begin at about 11:00 a.m. At the bottom of the second rappel, she missed the correct anchors and rappelled past them. She found some other fixed gear to clip into. She was about 50 feet to the climber's right of the correct anchors and a little bit below them. Her partner rappelled to the correct anchors and after talking to each other about what to do, they decided to have him pull the ropes and try to swing over to her. Once they pulled the ropes, they could not swing the ropes over to her location and her partner did not have any of the climbing gear. She had the rack and most of their extra clothes. For two hours, they tried unsuccessfully to get the ropes to her. Her climbing partner rappelled the rest of the way down and went for help. He located RMNP trail crew on Longs Peak who notified the Park.

A team of four Rangers was flown to the summit of Longs Peak just before dark. They down climbed Kiener's Route to Table ledge and lowered a Ranger to the stranded climber. She was able to ascend the rope back to Table Ledge. From there one of the Rangers escorted her to the summit. They arrived at the summit at 2:15 a.m. The climber and the Rangers bivied on the summit until 7:00 a.m. Between 7:00 a.m. and 10:00 a.m., the Rangers collected all the gear and a helicopter flew all the personnel, the climber, and their gear off the mountain.

Analysis

These climbers had years of alpine and big-wall experience and Ms. Davis had done this route the previous year. They started early, climbed efficiently, had the proper equipment, and they were on their way back down with time to spare. Once they became separated and got off of the standard rappel route, they discussed a plan that would get them back on the route together. Unfortunately this plan did not succeed.

More than likely, fatigue (these climbers had been walking/climbing since 1:30 a.m.) played a large role in helping to convince them that their plan could work. It certainly must have seemed easier than the other options of having her ascend the rope or building their own anchors and leaving gear behind to get back to Broadway. Fortunately, the stranded climber had rain gear and extra clothes and could endure the several rainstorms that occurred that afternoon while she waited for a rescue team to arrive. (Source: Rich Browne, Emergency Services Coordinator, Rocky Mountain National Park)

FALL ON ROCK, ROCKSLIDE
Colorado, Mount Wilson, El Diente Traverse

During the morning of July 26, a group of seven climbers were traversing the ridge between Mount Wilson (14,246 feet) and El Diente (14,159 feet) peaks, one of Colorado's four classic 14'er traverses.

According to reports, a group of four climbers Peter Topp (59), Charlie Zimmerman (60), Kathy (36), and Shawn Sullivan were on their way from Mount Wilson to meet with three unidentified climbers who had reached the summit of El Diente. The three were heading toward the others when they heard the sound of falling rocks and cries for help.

During the ensuing rockslide, Topp was rendered unconscious and later died from blunt force trauma to his head and body. Zimmerman sustained a head injury and internal injuries and with support was able to descend from 14,000 feet to a landing zone some 700 feet below. Kathy Donnelly had to be transported to the landing zone in a litter after dislocating and fracturing her hip in the accident. Shawn Sullivan was uninjured.

Members of the San Miguel Search and Rescue team were dropped off by helicopter about 800 vertical feet below the scene and had to climb to reach the climbers. The two injured climbers were lowered by rope systems to an area where a helicopter could make a safe landing. Rescuers had to wait out several hail and lightning storms that grounded the helicopters. (Source: Edited from postings on July 27 www.14ers.com)

RAPPEL ERROR – CARABINER GATE NOT CLOSED, NO HARD HAT
Colorado, Boulder Canyon, Boulderado Crag

On August 17, Andrew Tysinger (23) was on top of the Boulderado Crag with his girlfriend showing her how to rappel when he fell from the top of the crag. He was not wearing a helmet.

Andrew's girlfriend told rescuers that the carabiner gate on Andrew's harness was not properly closed when he first pushed off to begin his descent. It was estimated that Andrew fell 100 feet, coming into contact with several rocks and ledges before landing in the westbound lane of CO-119 near the 32-mile marker. (Source: Boulder County Sheriff's Department and www.dailycamera.com)

Analysis

Here is another case of not using equipment properly. Also at work here were inexperience and a bit of showing off. (Source: Editors)

ROCK GAVE AWAY – FALL ON ROCK
Colorado, Indian Peaks

On August 21, Glenn Porzak (64), his son Austin Porzak, and Robert Petrowsky were climbing on the East Ridge between Little Pawnee Peak (12,466 feet) and Pawnee Peak (12,943 feet). Sometime during the morning, Glenn fell and suffered serious injuries.

Robert said the fall happened while the group was on a low fifth-class rock face when a rock gave way as Glenn was climbing down. Robert stated that he saw Glenn tumble down with additional rocks falling around him and then he went out of sight. Robert then ran down the trail to summon rescuers while Austin went down to help his father.

Once rescuers reached Glenn and Austin around noon, they found him on a steep 50 to 60 degree scree slope at approximately 12,000 feet and that Glenn had fallen approximately 60–70 feet and had sustained significant injuries. Per one RMRG member on scene, it was going to be a "multi-pitch, all-day event" to evacuate Glenn off the scree slope. Rescuers on scene worked to medically stabilize Glenn and to place him in a litter for evacuation. Rescue crews had to rig up a technical rope rescue that involved six pitches to get down to walk-able terrain (almost 1,200 feet down). The effort was hampered by significant loose rock and a lot of rockfall. Rescuers were able to evacuate Glenn to a suitable landing area, where a Blackhawk military helicopter ferried him to another landing site near Brainard Lake. A Flight For Life then flew Glenn to St. Anthony Central Hospital. (Source: Boulder County Sheriff's Department Press Release)

FALL ON ROCK, PROTECTION PULLED OUT
Colorado, Eldorado Canyon State Park

On August 21, 2010, Donald Budlong fell from the slippery crux on the Bastille Crack (5.7+) and pulled two pieces, the highest of which was placed in the large flake to the right of the actual crack. He suffered a broken pelvis and other injuries.

Analysis

Stemming across from the big hollow flake to the actual Bastille Crack is not very uniform. The crack widens as it goes deeper into the formation. Most climbers place gear at this point and take the time to check to be sure that the placement is in a spot where it won't walk deeper into the crack. (Source: From a post on mountainproject.com)

FALL ON ROCK — LOOSE ROCK, CLIMBING UNROPED, CLIMBING ALONE
Colorado, Rocky Mountain National Park, Longs Peak, The Diamond,

On August 27 at 8:00 a.m., two NPS Climbing Rangers on the third pitch of Yellow Wall on The Diamond heard rockfall and saw several large rocks and a person falling in the vicinity of Broadway Ledge (a large ledge at the base of the Diamond) near the top of the North Chimney (the 800 foot, 5.6 approach climb that leads to Broadway). Benjamin Hebb (26), an experienced climber, fell down the North Chimney onto the Mills Glacier sustaining fatal injuries. The Rangers rappelled 1600 feet down the Yellow Wall and down the Lower East face to the body. Meanwhile another Ranger on patrol in the area had also arrived at the scene. Hebb's body was flown off the glacier with a helicopter.

During the resulting investigation Rangers determined that this climber had been attempting to aid-solo the Dunn-Westbay (grade V, 5.8, A3) route on the Diamond. He had started early that morning and soloed up the North Chimney to the base of this route. He likely had just started climbing up the route when he pulled a loose rock off and fell to his death. His rope was still in his pack when he was found.

Analysis

Even though no one will ever know the full story behind this tragic incident, it is likely that this climber's fall resulted from loose rock. This experienced climber had the necessary equipment to complete his intended route. He chose not to rope up for the North Chimney and the easy terrain near the start of the climb. This is not an uncommon choice for climbers on The Diamond where every second wasted means a much greater chance for being caught in a storm. Making the choice to forego a partner for the entire climb and a rope for part of it heightens the consequences of a slip or fall. A climber choosing to climb in this fashion must be sure of every move and every hold. Alpine routes have an abundance of objective hazards and loose rock will always exist even on a wall as popular as The Diamond. (Source: Rich Browne, Emergency Services Coordinator, Rocky Mountain National Park and http://climbinglife.com)

(Editors' Note: There were a few other incidents on Longs Peak this year, including a classic afternoon lightning strike, a solo climber, 28, who took 150-foot fall because he had no technical gear for the conditions, and a 57-year-old man who took a fatal 300-foot fall from The Ledges. No details on the latter.)

FALL ON ROCK, CARABINER IMPALED IN ARM
Colorado, Eldorado Canyon State Park

On September 4, Patrick Kadel (age unknown) was climbing Break On Through (5.11) when he fell seconding the first pitch. Before the belayer could stop his fall, Kadel somehow impaled his right forearm into the rope-end carabiner of a point of protection. According the victim, his fall was stopped by hanging from the carabiner impaled in his forearm. The climbers rappelled and walked out to the road with the carabiner still impaled in Kadel's forearm. The victim refused medical attention and an ambulance and was transported to a hospital in a private vehicle.

Analysis

This type of accident rarely occurs. This year, however, two reports of a carabiner impaling and/or lacerating an arm were reported (see North Carolina). Although the actual cause of both accidents is only speculation, climbers can prevent this type of incident by not grabbing long slings during a fall and consider using locking carabiners on the rope-end of long draws. (Source: Steve Muehlhauser, Park Ranger, Eldorado Canyon State Park and Aram Attarian)

STRANDED, INADEQUATE EQUIPMENT, CLIMBING ALONE
Colorado, Second Flatiron

On September 4, rescuers were dispatched to the Second Flatiron on a report of a stranded climber. Noah Gershon (20) was located on a near vertical edge of the "Pullman Car," a rock feature on the upper portion of the Second Flatiron. Due to Gershon's location, it took almost two hours to reach and secure him. Gershon was then assisted to the summit, and hiked out to the trailhead under his own power. He was not injured.

Analysis

Gershon has some experience climbing and was "bouldering" on the edge of the Second Flatiron when he decided to climb the Flatiron's face. He was unfamiliar with the common routes and got into a situation where he was unable to climb further up and could not down-climb to easier terrain. Gershon had on rock climbing shoes, but did not have a harness, helmet or rope with him. (Source: Boulder County Sheriff's Department)

FALL ON ROCK, CLIMBING ALONE, INADEQUATE CLOTHING AND EQUIPMENT
Colorado, Boulder Canyon, Dome Rock

On the evening of September 9, Brenna Fisch (19), began soloing up The Owl (5.7), a popular crack climb on The Dome, a 200-foot-high granite cliff. From all indications, it appears that Brenna slipped, then slid and fell 40 feet down the cliff to the base at about 6:00 p.m., about an hour before sunset. She suffered multiple injuries, including a severe head injury, crushed eye socket and forehead. Slipping in and out of consciousness, she began crawling down the access path to a bike path below.

She managed to crawl about 100 feet. Two climbers found her twelve hours later at 6:30 a.m. the next morning. She was hypothermic. Brenna was dressed in spandex shorts, sports bra, and shoes and not prepared for the night's cold temperatures. She was evacuated by rescuers and transported to Boulder Community Hospital where surgeons repaired her skull, rebuilt her eye socket, and reattached an ear. (Source: http://climbing.about.com)

STRANDED, EXCEEDING ABILITIES, INEXPERIENCE, INADEQUATE CLOTHING/EQUIPMENT
Colorado, Rocky Mountain National Park, Longs Peak, Keiner's Route

On September 2, a party of two men (ages 53 and 34) with no alpine rock or any snow/ice experience attempted Keiner's Route on Longs Peak. (Keiner's is a 2,000-foot, grade II, AI 2, 5.3–5.5 route.) This route starts with an 800-foot snow/ice couloir known as Lambs Slide then finishes with 1,200 feet of alpine rock, with climbing ranging from 4th class to 5.5. This party encountered more difficult and time consuming climbing than expected while attempting this route. After spending six and a half hours climbing the snow/ice couloir, they started up the rock section at about 3:00 p.m. They managed to climb about four pitches over the next four and a half hours, but could not find climbing that they thought was easier than 5.8. They reached a point that they could not continue from and ended rappelling back to an exposed ledge where they spent the night resting and running in place to stay warm. The next morning they called the NPS for help and stated that they were stranded. They could not find the way up and did not think that they could safely descend the snow/ice couloir. Park Rangers convinced them to reverse the route as far as they could while other Rangers climbed up to them. The Rangers assisted them off the route by climbing with them up Lamb's Slide to the large saddle between Mount Meeker and Longs Peak. After descending the third-class Loft route with the Rangers, these two climbers spent a second night in the backcountry at Chasm Shelter with Rangers and walked out unharmed the next morning.

Analysis

These two climbers had minimal climbing experience, and neither climber had any alpine rock or snow/ice climbing experience. One had just started climbing in a gym this winter and had only climbed outdoors twice before this trip. The other started climbing three years ago. Even though most of his experience also came from the gym, he has climbed some outdoors at places like Seneca, Red Rocks and the New River Gorge amongst others. He had done some multi-pitch traditional climbing before this trip.

They had not climbed grades harder than 5.5 in the gym and likely assumed that the 5.5 rating meant that this climb would be "easy" for them. They did not research or plan for a retreat route if something went wrong. Their escape plan involved programming the emergency number for Rocky Mountain National Park into a cell phone. Their lack of an honest personal assessment of their abilities put their own lives at risk as well as the lives of the Rangers who had to climb up to help them.

Even though they got themselves into this situation, they did make several good decisions once they realized that they could not complete the route. They did not blindly push forward on the route, but instead they began to retreat to a safer spot and elected to spend the night there. Once they contacted Rangers, they safely made their way to a meeting point. They accurately assessed their own inability to safely descend Lambs Slide.

Overall this party could have prevented their own rescue in several ways. Here are two of the most obvious: (1) They could have simply chosen another, less committing, route to start their alpine climbing career—one that matched their abilities more closely. A route like the North Face route on Longs Peak would have still allowed them to summit Longs Peak; however, it would have been within their ability. Some discussions with Rangers in the Longs Peak Ranger Station or more preplanning could have pointed them in this direction. (2) More research on the possible escape routes from Keiner's would have allowed them more chances of affecting their own rescue. If they had known that they could have continued up Lambs Slide to the Loft and then walked down, then they likely would have used this option. (Source: Edited from a report by Rich Browne, Park Ranger Emergency Services Coordinator, Rocky Mountain National Park)

FALL ON ROCK, PRE-EXISTING CONDITION
Colorado, Eldorado Canyon State Park, Redgarden Wall

On Saturday, September 25 Maria Petzolt (26) dislocated her shoulder unexpectedly while pulling on a hold on the fourth pitch of Ruper (5.8), a 6-pitch route on the Redgarden Wall. Maria had dislocated the same shoulder five weeks earlier on another outing. Her male climbing partner lowered her to a secure position a few feet lower and called 911 on his cell phone. When rescuers arrived, they administered medication and reduced the shoulder after a few attempts. Ms. Petzolt was tandem-lowered to the base of the wall. She refused an ambulance and was transported to a hospital in a private vehicle. (Source: Steve Muehlhauser, Park Ranger, Eldorado Canyon State Park)

Analysis

Many people have a pre-disposition to spontaneous shoulder dislocations. If a climber knows about this, he or she can compensate by taking care on how far to reach and how much leverage to exert. (Source: Jed Williamson)

FALL ON ICE/ SNOW, CLIMBING UNROPED, POOR CONDITIONS
Colorado, Rocky Mountain National Park, Taylor Glacier

On October 16, a party of three started up the Taylor Glacier. The Taylor Glacier is a 40–60 degree 1,500-foot permanent snowfield in Rocky Mountain National Park. Two weeks prior, James Patrick (54), the leader of the group had attempted the route and turned around due to poor snow conditions and black ice. Also, it would have been hard to ignore the late season conditions that exposed much loose rock and dirt inside the couloir. Now, the glacier was partially covered with ten inches of snow that had fallen 5 days prior. It was the first measurable snowfall of the year and did not bond well to the existing layer of black ice nor did it do more than barely cover up the loose rock and dirt. Starting up the route at first light and climbing unroped, the first 1,000 feet of the route went easily as they were able to stay in the main couloir and avoid sections of black ice and loose rock. At this point, the party took a break and discussed options: to continue in the main couloir and climb the steep headwall or break left on a weakness that appeared to be easier.

The party chose to follow the left line because it looked easier. Encountering a few short steep steps, one member of the party felt uneasy, and another member belayed her using a long piece of webbing. The going became a little slower as the party had to navigate around patches of black ice and carefully cross steep sections of loose rock that were covered with only a few inches of snow.

With the group's only rope in his backpack, the leader of the group chose to continue soloing the final steep headwall before exiting onto the ridge. As he climbed the 50–60 degree headwall that was covered by patches of black ice and unconsolidated snow atop of dirt, he slipped. He slid about 30 feet before disappearing out of view. The two remaining climbers anchored themselves to the wall using two ice screws and an ice ax and used a radio to call for help. The party reported that they were stuck, "…fifty to 100 feet from the top," and that their partner had taken, "…a fall of at least 200 feet." Within a few hours, Rangers were able to assist the two climbers to the safety and determine that the leading climber had fallen 1,500 feet to his death.

Analysis

The two climbers made a wise decision to stay put and wait for help after their partner's fall. Many climbers choose to solo this type of alpine terrain because it is "easy" and finding anchors can be time consuming. This, like most classic alpine terrain, is not difficult, but it can be dangerous. Although recently improved, the route was still in very poor climbing conditions. The poor conditions also attributed to the fact that protection was not easily available, thus negating the use of a rope. The snow climbing guidebook that the group consulted notes itself as "A Guide for all Seasons" and lists this route, along with other similar objectives in Rocky Mountain National Park, as best from "summer into autumn," and lists October as the best time to climb. In a normal year, climbers encounter black ice and loose rock on most of the park's permanent snowfields from late August to October. These are some of the least desirable times to snow climb and previous trips along with a visual analysis of the day's conditions should have clued the climbers into the fact that conditions were not ideal, as their guidebook stated. (Source: Rich Browne, Emergency Services Coordinator, Rocky Mountain National Park)

STUCK RAPPEL ROPE, FALL ON ROCK, INADEQUATE EQUIPMENT – BOOTS
Colorado, Boulder Canyon, Bihedral Wall

Beth M. Davis (52) fell while trying to retrieve a stuck rappel rope after climbing in Boulder Canyon on October 31. Davis and her partner were rappelling on the Upper Bihedral Wall. Once on the ground, they began to pull the rope. The rope became stuck on a spot roughly halfway up the rappel route. Davis scrambled up the rock to free it, and in the process fell approximately 20 feet. She suffered a broken arm and possibly a broken shoulder and internal injuries from the fall. Rocky Mountain Rescue Group was able to stabilize and evacuate her. She was transported by helicopter to St. Anthony's Central in Denver.

Analysis

Ms. Davis comments on her accident: "The main thing I want to say is that wearing my helmet was the smartest thing I did that day. I have no spinal or head injuries. In retrospect, I made several mistakes. I knew my shoes were very inappropriate for hiking much less free climbing. I did not adequately assess the situation nor did I consider any other options. I fell because my foot slipped. Don't put saving time or inconvenience ahead of being safe. Another method or assistance from others should have been considered". (Source: From numerous posts on Mountainproject.com)

FALL ON ICE, INADEQUATE PROTECTION – MISSED BACK-UP CHECK AND WARNING, HASTE
Colorado, Rocky Mountain National Park, Thatchtop Mountain

On November 20, as my friend Chris Pruchnic (42) and I walked early in the morning to our original destination, the Black Lake Slabs or West Gully ice climbs in RMNP, we talked at length. Chris, about running—a 100 mile race which he had completed about a month before, as Front Range Section Chair of the American Alpine Club—the recent Lumpy Ridge Trail work day which he had helped to organize and both of us had participated in, his upcoming climbing exchange trip to Iran, his guiding services—climbing trips to South America and SCUBA trips. He said he had not climbed as much as he had wanted last year. I talked mostly about work and rock and ice climbing.

Once we arrived at Mills Lake, Chris wanted to aim for a route called All Mixed Up (AMU) on Thatchtop Mountain. AMU and a route on the right looked like it was in good shape but since we had brought no rock gear I said, "It would be nice to have at least a set of stoppers," and pointed out an area called Reflections. He brought our attention back to the AMU wall, which appeared well formed to the right and center. The left side looked very thin and mostly dry. We looked it over more closely and thought that it had enough ice to avoid having to do much climbing on rock if we stayed to the middle standard line of AMU. When I asked him about West Gully, he confirmed that he had led the crux pitch of West Gully a few years before so he was more inclined to do something new. "What do you think?" he said. I had a printed out topo of West Gully but I didn't have one of AMU. I had looked over route topos and descriptions many times over the years. Apparently Chris had been researching the route in the recent days before and had his sights set on it and was convinced that we could do the route with screws only. I thought so as well. We agreed to do the center route on the AMU wall and started up the approach.

It was a windy day, but we were on the lee side so communication was not a problem. We geared up, did a complete safety check, and I led the first pitch up to the left end of the rocky headwall and stopped at a fixed belay station. He seconded up and we quickly exchanged gear. As he was about to start up the second pitch, I offered to take the tagline from him, but because it was so light he kept it on his back. Starting out with a couple of steps on verglas then good ice for a short section, the pitch turned to tricky low angle verglas and frozen sod. Enjoying the challenge, Chris yelled out, "It's mixed baby!" We were having a good time. He had led about half way up the second pitch when he said he saw a fixed anchor off to the left. I yelled back "The route goes back to the right!" to the standard center route with the fat ice we saw from Mills Lake.

He said, "I'm going to use it." He went left to a fixed anchor station on a ledge.

As I seconded up, again about halfway to where he was belaying, I noticed a fixed pin to the right and pointed out that we were probably off route. He said he'd completely missed that pin. I suggested that I could go right and set a belay so that he could down-climb and traverse over. The ice between his and my positions was good and not steep. There was at least one screw between us. He pointed out that there was another fixed pin further to the left and up from where he was. I couldn't see it, so I agreed to come up to where he was belaying and take a closer look with the condition that we could still go back right if I didn't like how the left side looked.

He had me on belay on an anchor of three pre-existing fixed points and runners, not from his harness. He was on the left side under two fixed pieces of webbing. The rope was flaked, looped from side to side across his three slings, which were clipped with lockers to the fixed gear. I believe one of his lockers connected the left two fixed slings to one on the right. When I came up to the ledge, I clipped in to the right side of the anchor on a fixed runner under a fixed pin with one of my locking 'biners and tied in with a clove hitch on my end of the rope. He pointed out the route to the left.

Chris commented that he was uncomfortable at his sloping stance as he fiddled with his lockers. He wanted to move to where I was standing on flatter ground. He had loosened the rings on his lockers but no red was showing. I was thinking that he wanted to step down next to me, on my left, by extending or moving one runner at a time. He was still anchored on all three points.

I looked over to the left and checked out the route. On an easy looking, mostly snowy traverse below a rock band, there was a fixed pin about 30+ feet out. The band was mostly a slab, running above the traverse. Another 30 feet or so from the pin, there was what appeared from our angle to be a 3–4-foot wide smear of ice on the slab, detached on the edges. It looked only inches thick. Fifteen feet above the start of the smear I couldn't see anything. (A photo showed it to be all rock, topos show no named route)

At this time he said, "So I noticed that you tied the rope directly into the anchor with a clove hitch. I'd like to start using it more quickly and efficiently. It's not that I can't tie one; it's just not a knot that I use very often. So how do you... or before you show me let me just do it. Rather than look through all this rope (in front of him), I'll just use your end." He tried once, didn't look right. Tried again, no good. Tried something different, not as good as the previous time. Once again same result. "Oh that's embarrassing!" he said, frustrated.

I took the bight of rope from him and said, "Ok look. Here's how I tie it. I just..." I showed him how I do it. I handed the rope back to him without the knot. He tied it right. First try that time.

Me: "That's it." Chris: "That's it."

I looked to my right and thought it still wouldn't be that much work to get back on the original route. I heard 'biners clipping so I looked back left to see that Chris was in the process of removing the third of his lockers. When he took his pieces off unannounced to move to a better stance, he left me on only one fixed pin. I knew that I hadn't checked for a fourth backup, so I said emphatically, "Wait what are you doing? Clip back in!!" As he stepped behind me, he disregarded my warning saying, "It's easier to move all of it at the same time." It was too late for me to restrain him physically, so I stood still so as not to disrupt his movements. I felt his hand slide down my back as he said, "Oops!" At that point pure wishful thinking overtook my mind and I looked to my right and said: "Chris?" Chris said: "What?"

I thought he had responded to me, but instead I'm now sure he was wondering when his knot was going to catch. Gear rattled. I looked left and right. From then on I couldn't make out anything he said. I said, "Where'd you go?" Oh God, I thought. I finally turned around far enough to catch just a glimpse of where he was and was shocked at how far he had fallen. Me: "CHRIS!!!"

I had to turn back forward, pull on gear and re-adjust my feet to get a better look straight below and behind me. As I was doing so, I heard the loud impact. He must have been in the air a good distance and hit hard.

When I was able to turn far enough around to get a good look, he was sliding fast down a lower angle section and finally came to a sudden stop. The anchor clanged and shook as I turned back up to see that we were both on only that one piton and only two knots between us. His clove hitch had caught, but he had tied it on my end of the rope. He'd forgotten that he hadn't looked for his end of the rope. It seemed to me that he was simply practicing the hitch, not about to rely on it as a backup. I stared at the pin and wondered: Well..., was I supposed to go with him? It would be easier to deal with that, than to have to go through this. I was completely stunned.

I noticed that the rope had stopped his fall above a snow ledge. I tested the tension on the rope and found that it was fully weighted. His weight shifted to one side and then no movement after that. Although there was only a small chance he could have survived the fall and that he was unconscious, I had to at least assume that he was alive. I continually called out to him.

I took a minute to collect myself, assessing what was possible. I backed up my anchor to the other two fixed slings. It was about 12:00 p.m. I had ample gear, but no tagline, and a weighted lead line with a tangled knot on the lower half of the rope. No one else was on the route. I didn't have a phone on me. The chances of a rescue before nightfall were remote.

My choices were to solo down the route, descend the weighted line with prusiks or utilize the ten feet or so that I could work into the system. I looked carefully at his position above the ledge. It was a sloping ledge and he could have continued to slide if I were able to work in the additional slack to lower him. He seemed to be close enough above it for me to invest the time to find out. I rigged a very basic hauling system and was able to lift his weight off the hitch. I untied from my end of the rope and tied it to the lowest point, freed the hitches and lowered him to the ledge where he settled into the snow.

As long as he didn't slide, I could rap down to him. I cleaned the belay device and locker that he'd left and the rest of my gear and carefully started rappelling down, trying not to dislodge him. As I was working on passing the knot, I sensed that he was gone and prepared myself for the worst. He had never responded to my calls. Shortly before I reached him, I saw that he was caught in the rope loops. When I got to the ledge I found he had no signs of life and knew he had departed long before I could reach him. It was about 12:40 p.m. I stayed with him for a while. Then keeping the scene as intact as possible, I retrieved the tag line and continued rappelling to the base.

I was told the coroner's report says he lasted only seconds after the end of the fall. During one of my interviews with the rangers, I asked RMNP SAR Director Ranger Mark Pita, "Why did he do that? Why did he ignore my warning? Who does that?" He responded: "He had his mind set."

Analysis

Check and double-check your anchors. Announce your intention and don't make a move until all questions are resolved with your partner. Focus on one thing at a time. You could also say don't take your eyes off your partner, but then you wouldn't be watching what you yourself are doing, much less scoping the route, keeping an eye on the weather or hazards, etc. (Source: Jean Wilks)

FALL ON ROCK, INADEQUATE BELAY — ROPE PULLS THROUGH BELAY DEVICE
Colorado, Eldorado Canyon State Park

On December 14, a female climber (27) was lowered off the end of her rope after leading the first pitch of Over the Hill (5.10). Drew Wojcik was in the climbing party directly above her and recounts what he saw: "As we began the second pitch of Over the Hill we heard the fall. Initially it sounded like a scary leader fall, but soon found out that was not the case. I instantly lowered my leader who asked if help was needed. He observed the rope running through the new bolted anchors that have replaced using the tree. We estimate she fell around 20 feet to the ground. Initial assessment seemed to indicate a hip injury. The party involved seemed fairly new to the area, referencing our guidebook. The new anchors are probably around 70m."

Analysis

Moral of the story is tie-in or [have a] back-up. I think the Eldo fixed hardware committee should consider tagging some of the more traveled moderates that involve raps/lowers longer than can be done with a 50 or 60m. Seems like this is a recurring issue after speaking with the rescue team. (Source: From a post on http://www.mountainproject.com/)

STRANDED, POOR RAPPEL TECHNIQUE
Colorado, Flatirons

During the morning of On December 28, Kevin Mines (53) and his son (16) started climbing the Third Flatiron. Later in the day while descending, Kevin injured his back rappelling and was unable to hike out. He called for assistance via cell phone at 10:16 p.m.

Kevin recounts his misadventure: "We roped up and started climbing about 10:45 a.m. I had climbed the Third Flatiron four times before, the last time in 1998. My son had limited climbing experience but was willing to try the Third since the forecast predicted good weather. We talked about swapping leads, but after the first pitch, my son decided that he'd rather second the entire route.

"We made slow and steady progress and reached the top of our climb by about 4:45 p.m. By now it was getting dark and we had been dealing with strong cold winds that picked up during the late afternoon. We decided to skip the final summit pitch and instead tried to maneuver our way through the boulders up to the base of the first standard rappel and the start of the second rappel. On our way we encountered a large, smooth, 12-foot boulder. My son was able to surmount this obstacle by using my back and shoulders for footholds. He in turn belayed me up the obstacle.

"By now it was dark and with headlamps on we began our descent. The prospect of rappelling in the dark was a bit frightening, especially for my son. On the 50-foot rappel to Friday's Folly Ledge I found myself descending too fast and somewhat out of control, but made it OK. My son followed with perfect form. We spent some time here deciding between the 75-foot rappel around the corner or the 140-foot rappel from where we were. We decided on the longer rappel.

"For this rappel I switched from a standard ATC to a Guide ATC which has a high friction mode. During my rappel, I was concentrating on the friction and trying to descend at a slow, safe speed. Suddenly, my feet went out of control and I flipped upside down. This action was probably the first instance of injury to my back. I tried unsuccessfully to maneuver to a normal rappel position. I was able to keep my brake hand on the ropes and continued the rappel another 100 feet bouncing around upside down/ sideways and landing on the ground flat on my back!

"I could feel the pain in my lower back (two previous back surgeries in the late 90s). I was happy to be on the ground and because of my back injury, couldn't move for about ten minutes. I called up to my son to wait a few minutes. Eventually I forced myself to roll over, got up and unclipped the rope so my son could rappel. He joined me on the ground at approximately 8:30 p.m.

"Despite the pain, I was able to get up and walk around a little on flat terrain. In order to continue our descent, we had to hike up a 30-foot low angle wall. Normally this wouldn't be a huge problem, but with my injury I tried twice from two different sides and made it halfway. We rested for a while and called my wife in Lafayette and my oldest son in Montana, a professional mountain guide, to seek advice. We wanted to self-rescue and hike out but decided instead to call 911 a little after 10:00 p.m."

A total of thirty-five rescuers worked for more than eight hours to get the pair out. Mines was transported to Boulder Community Hospital with non-life threatening injuries. His son was uninjured.

Analysis

"In hindsight, there were some things that we should have done differently: Attempted a shorter climb, started earlier since we knew we were slow, pushed harder, practiced rappelling in advance, and familiarized ourselves with rappel safeguards (e.g. prusik, etc.)." (Source: Edited from a post by Kevin Mines on mountainproject.com)

(Editors' Note: We did not post all the "fall on rock" narratives available, as the half-dozen others we were sent or we found on line included similar causes.)

FALL ON ROCK, PROTECTION PULLED
Georgia, Tallulah Gorge State Park

Joshua Robertson (20), an avid rock climber, died of injuries from a fall on April 20. He was climbing with three others. Sources said the fall happened on P2 of Mescaline Daydream (5.8) and that one or more gear placements failed. Joshua was not wearing a helmet. Park officials said this is the first climbing-related fatality since the park was established in 1993. (Source: www.ajc.com/news/uga)

INADEQUATE BELAY, FALL ON ROCK
Idaho, City of Rocks National Reserve, Parking Lot Rock

On August 19, Jeff Everett (49) was lowered off the end of his seventy-meter rope on "Delay of the Game."

He fell at least 20-30 meters, impacting ledges and a Mahogany tree on the way and landed on the ground. He sustained multiple injuries including a broken neck. Bystanders, City of Rocks staff, and local EMS were all involved in his care and transport to Twin Falls Idaho, where he was treated and released after five days.

Analysis

Jeff Everett is a very experienced climber. As to why his belayer dropped him is not stated. Tying in to both ends of the rope would have prevented this accident. (Source: From a report by Brad Schilling, Climbing Ranger)

INADEQUATE BELAY, FALL ON ROCK, NO HARD HAT
Idaho, City of Rocks National Reserve, Twist and Crawl

Twist and Crawl is about a 35–39-meter route. The leader (53) of the route, clipped draws to the anchor chains and was to be lowered off. The belayer's (mid-50s) end of the rope wasn't tied to her and she let the 60-meter rope end slide through the device, resulting in the leader falling to the ground. He sustained lacerations, abrasions, a fracture, and a concussion.

Analysis

Tying in to both ends of the rope would have prevented this accident. The use of a helmet might have lessened the severity of the worst injury.

(Editor's Note: There were two other incidents from City, but they were minor in nature. There was one other report from Idaho this year. Two young men were off-route on Sturs Chimney on Mount Heyburn in the Sawtooth Wilderness area when one of them fell about 50 feet, resulting in a sprain and fracture. The good news is that they negotiated the terrain, including many miles of hobbling. They made it out in time to prevent the SAR effort that had been initiated.)

NO EXPERIENCE – SOLO CLIMBING, INADEQUATE EQUIPMENT FALL ON ROCK
Kentucky, Red River Gorge, Beachcomber

On February 13, Shaun Wilhoite (28) was camping in the area with a large group of friends. The group hiked to Pebble Beach around 2:00 p.m. Upon arriving, Shaun began to free-solo Beachcomber (5.4) in leather hiking boots. His friends said he had no rock climbing experience. When he started climbing, the rest tried to stop him but he did not listen. After topping out, he moved over onto the Arrowhead Pinnacle, from which he fell about 54 feet, headfirst, onto the rock-strewn base. His three best friends tried to revive him, but he had apparently died instantly.

RRGMRT responded and performed the recovery. Resuscitation attempts at the scene were unsuccessful. (Source: From a post on redriverclimbing.com)

FALL ON ROCK
Kentucky, Red River Gorge

On April 17 M. Tucker was climbing above bolt three when he fell approximately 30–40 feet while climbing Elephant Man (5.13b). He suffered fatal head injuries. (Source: Edited from: www.redriverclimbing.com

FALL ON ROCK, ROPE SEVERED BY CARABINER
Kentucky, Red River Gorge, Midnight Surf Wall

In early September, an experienced climber (age unknown) on Tape Worm (5.12d) took a lead fall from a point between the first and second bolt. His rope ran from his belay, through a quickdraw hanging from the first bolt, to his harness. On this particular route, the first bolt is located high enough that he would not have decked under normal circumstances. Unfortunately, when he fell, his rope was completely severed by the lower carabiner on the quickdraw attached to the first bolt, and he did deck. He sustained head injuries and is on his way to a full recovery.

Analysis

The quickdraw in question is comprised of two Trango carabiners marked: "Trango Italy." The CE 0638 rating on each 'biner is 24 kilo-Newtons in line with the spine and four kilo-Newtons perpendicular to the spine. (This is the older style classic wire 'biner made in Italy—not the newer design made in Korea.) The two 'biners are connected with a Petzl dogbone (strap between the two 'biners) rated at 22 kilo-Newtons. The quickdraw was removed from the first bolt of "Tape Worm" shortly after the accident. It was found to be intact and operable, but the two 'biners were severely worn by the actions of a climbing rope being pulled through the bottom 'biner and the hanger bracket grinding away on the top one. It is not known who hung this quickdraw or when it was hung. The carabiner in question was never intended to be permanently hung on a popular route and expected to withstand numerous leader falls. Sand-laden ropes serve as a very effective abrasive cutting tool and can wear down lightweight aluminum carabiners in a relatively short period of time. Quickdraws have been left hanging on several overhanging routes in the Red, as well as other climbing venues, over the years by developers and climbers. There are no routine inspections of hardware performed on Red routes. Climbing visitors are warned to trust *absolutely nothing* they find fixed to climbing routes. Check fixed gear before committing to it! If a 'biner is grooved and (most of all) sharp, take it off the route and replace it with a new one!

Follow-up: All quickdraws having aluminum carabiners have been removed from climbs in Muir Valley and new stainless steel PermaDraws (by Climb Tech) have been installed in their places by volunteers. (Source: Rick & Liz Weber, from a post on redriverclimbing.com)

FALL ON ROCK, NO HARD HAT
Kentucky, Red River Gorge

As is usually the case, Breakfast Burrito (5.10d) had a line of climbers waiting for it on June 6, and when she finally had a chance, CL (age unknown) took her turn on Breakfast Burrito. CL and another member of our group set up, stick clipped the first bolt, and then I came over and put CL on belay. I stood just to her right, at the base of the wall under the first bolt. She started up the route, hung the second draw, repositioned, and as she reached for slack to clip, her left hand slipped off of her hold and she came crashing to the ground. She landed on her back on a flat boulder, her head just at its edge. Her eyes rolled back in her head, she seized, and only moments after impact, a stream of blood flowed from the back of her head!

With a nurse on site CL was stabilized until the ambulance arrived. Most improbably, she sustained only a minor laceration and sizable bump on her back and some lingering head and body aches.

Analysis

There are several precautions that could have been taken to prevent such an accident: stick-clipping the second bolt, spotting the climber, belayer being prepared to take in a lot of slack in a hurry by jumping off of something, first and second bolt being located nearer to each other. In retrospect, I wish CL had a helmet on her head, that I had been spotting her, and that the second bolt had been stick clipped. Any of these things could have made a serious difference, but the procedure we followed is typical, and the one I most often see being followed by others at The Red. Almost everyone knows the dangers of clipping the second bolt, including CL, and her hand slipping was unexpected. As she said, she was not excessively nervous or pumped.

This has been a lesson to me to never climb something, or allow someone else to climb something, if there is a potential for a ground fall, because there are always factors for which one cannot account. (Source: From a post on www.redriverclimbing.com)

FALL ON ROCK, INADEQUATE BELAY, DISTRACTION
Kentucky, Red River Gorge, Military Wall

A large group was gathered at Military Wall on September 12 playing music, possibly loud enough to make communication between climber and belayer difficult. Climber was getting into the upper knee bar on Reliquary (5.12b) when he fell near the last bolt. The climber landed on the belayer's dog, killing it instantly.

The belayer was holding the GriGri in her right hand with fingers over the cam-gri preventing it from locking and said she didn't know how it could have happened. Worse yet, she said this was the third time it has happened to her.

Analysis

Crags are becoming more crowded and distractions occur. Music, dogs, kids, cats, bears, etc. Pay attention to the climber! That person's life is in your hands! And don't pick up a belay device if you don't have proper training. (Source: From a post on www.redriverclimbing.com)

FALLING ROCK, POOR POSITION
Kentucky, Red River Gorge, Muir Valley

On October 19, a climber (age unknown) lounging on a boulder under a route at the Solarium was struck in the head and shoulder by a rock that had been dislodged by a climber above on an overhanging route. The injured party was given first aid treatment and delivered to an ambulance outside the Valley. (Source: From a post on www.redriverclimbing.com)

FALL ON ROCK
Kentucky, Red River Gorge, Roadside Crag

On November 20, a climber (age unknown) on Ro Shampo (5.12a) "smashed" their belayer into the boulder below the climb because they forgot to unclip the belay end of the rope after cleaning bolt #1 and taking the swing. (Source: From a post on www.redriverclimbing.com)

(Editor's Note: With the many Web sites devoted to climbing now in existence, we are learning more than we want to know about the kinds of errors climbers are making as a result of inexperience.)

FALL ON SNOW, FAULTY USE OF CRAMPONS, UNABLE TO SELF-ARREST
New Hampshire, Mount Washington, Lion Head

On March 6, a hiker was descending the steep section of Lion Head trail when snow had balled up in his crampons and he fell approximately 50 feet, injuring his lower leg. While bystanders began to haul him down the trail, the Snow Ranger that was returning to Hermit Lake from the first incident rerouted to respond to the incident. The patient's injuries were stabilized and he was transported to Pinkham Notch by snowmobile as well.

Analysis

The Lion Head Winter Route is a steep trail where conditions change quickly from day to day or even during the course of a single day. We recommend that an ice ax for safer travel on this route. (This assumes the ability to use this equipment properly.). In this instance, the patient had ski poles rather than an ice ax. For the purposes of arresting a fall in steep terrain, an ice ax is a far more effective tool than just regular ski poles. Self-arrest ski poles, such as Black Diamond's Whippet would serve as a good compromise.

Wearing crampons on descent in the kind of snow that will ball up is not recommended. If the snow is firm enough to use crampons on descent, then the climber will be facing sideways or in. (Source: www.mountwashingtonavalanchecenter.org and Jed Williamson)

FALL ON ICE, PROTECTION PULLED OUT
New Hampshire, Mount Washington, Pinnacle Gully

On March 20, a group of three climbers fell while simul-climbing upper pitches of Pinnacle Gully. It was a very busy Saturday in Huntington Ravine. Temperatures Friday were warm and sunny, and then overnight they stayed above the freezing mark. Saturday was also warm and sunny, so there was a significant amount of water running over the snow and ice in the gully. One party of two had climbed the first pitch and was preparing to rappel off due to the excessive water. Another party, including a local guide (KM) and his two clients had also climbed the first pitch, but rather than contend with the water, the guide climbed out of the gully on the rock to the right. As this was going on, the party of three was simul-climbing from the top of the first pitch (they had used traditional belays for the first pitch). DH was leading, TV was in the middle of the 60-meter rope, and GT was tied into the bottom end.

Between the top of the first pitch and the top of the climb, DH had seven pieces of protection: one fixed piton, four ice screws, a V-thread left by another party, and an ice ax deeply sunk and tied off. Just as DH was about to exit the gully, he felt the slack in the rope tighten up. After waiting a moment and not getting more slack to move upward, he stepped down a bit into a good stance to give slack to the climbers below him. At this time, TV had ascended to the second ice screw; GT had passed and unclipped the piton and V-thread but had not yet arrived at the first screw. As she was at the second screw and after unclipping it, TV began to have problems with her crampon falling off. After a couple minutes without much progress, GT began to climb up to assist her. This created a lot of slack between the bottom two climbers. TV eventually fell, pulling DH out of his stance near the top of the gully. He said that it happened very quickly, so he didn't really know what was happening. The ice tool and two screws above TV were ripped out of the ice and the two climbers began falling simultaneously down the gully. The fall was stopped by a single 10-cm ice screw that was between GT and TV. Had this screwed pulled out as well, it is likely that all three climbers would have fallen over the first pitch and possibly brought down other climbers with them.

According to the two clients of KM, DH fell down the left side of the gully and near the bottom hit the rocks, bouncing him across to the other side and missing them by only a few feet. The two came to rest near the top of the first pitch, having fallen approximately 300 feet (DH) and 100 feet (TV). Neither climber was seriously injured. KM quickly responded, assisting the entire group down off of the climb and stayed with them until out of the steep terrain in Huntington Ravine. Snow Rangers learned of the incident from the HMC caretaker who had heard about it from someone else. The climbers were encountered descending the trail to Pinkham Notch. They were bruised and slightly bloody otherwise uninjured and they walked themselves to the bottom.

Analysis

She commented afterward that she didn't really know what to do and probably should have clipped directly into the screw or even re-clipped the rope. (Source: www.mountwashingtonavalanchecenter)

FALL ON ROCK
New York, Adirondacks, Upper Washbowl Cliff

On August 16, Dennis Murphy (35) had reached the top of a climbing route on Upper Washbowl Cliffs in Keene Valley at about 6:10 p.m. when he lost his footing and fell more than 100 feet. New York State forest rangers and Keene Fire Department Wilderness Rescue personnel found Murphy near the bottom of the rock face.

Department of Environmental Conservation spokesman David Winchell said Murphy climbed up either Hesitation or Weissner. "Dennis, from what I understand, was a very good climber," Winchell said. Murphy and a companion had planned to rappel down Partition, a descent with a fixed anchor for the ropes. "There was an obstacle that he was walking around while his partner was tying off. Dennis came around this obstacle and slipped and fell." (Source: Edited from a report by Kim Smith Dedham and Michelle Besaw, *Keene-Valley News*)

(Editor's Note: Perhaps failing to be anchored in contributed to this fall. It is all too common to untie once at the top while preparing anchors to rappel or belay.)

FALL ON ROCK, PROTECTION PULLED OUT, EXCEEDING ABILITIES
New York, Mohonk Preserve, Shawangunks

On the morning of October 17, I (Lisa Wang, 23) was leading the route Frogs Head. It was my second day of leading at the 'Gunks.

At the bulge above the first crux, I first placed one small Metolius 1 and slung it with a long quickdraw. Next, I placed a gold nut about three to four feet up and put that on another quickdraw; however, I didn't like this placement very much and so placed a red nut about a foot immediately above the previous nut. This red nut was slotted into a v-shaped crevice, again slung with a quickdraw. At this point, I am approximately 40 feet up, possibly a little higher. When I was preparing to go up for the next set of holds, I smeared with my right foot because I couldn't reach the next horizontal crack otherwise; however, my left hand came off the rock and I fell off the bulge. Both nuts pulled, one by one, and then force of the fall also pulled the Metolius 1 cam. My partner told me he felt each piece hold for a second and then pop. He also felt the brown Tri-cam catch and take up most of the force of the fall. I hit the ground as a result of rope stretch and bounced twice. I sprained my left ankle, scraped up my left leg, and hurt my wrist. It turns out I broke a bone in my wrist, but the break was on a fairly minor bone, so I actually kept climbing that weekend.

Analysis

While I am relatively new to climbing, I can comfortably lead 5.9 sport routes and can climb 5.10 routes, so it was reasonable to expect that Frogs Head, a 5.6, would go smoothly. My second, who is also my mentor, has as many years of experience as I've been alive and is a very competent and skilled teacher and climber. My rack had a full set of nuts, Black Diamond C4 cams from .3–3, a Metolius 1, a set of Tri-cams, and about seven extendable two-foot slings and five long 16-cm quickdraws.

I found Frogs Head to be a bit more difficult than expected, partly because I am 5'1", so the holds were actually not within my grasp if I used the usual footholds. I believe that I fell back at the bulge and the horizontal force I exerted on my nut pulled it up and out. I also believe my Metolius 1 was under-cammed. When deciding whether to use slings or quickdraws, I decided that draws were sufficient because the route went pretty much straight up and thus there wouldn't be an horizontal rope drag. However, I failed to consider the force that a draw would exert on a nut in the event of the fall and how the bulge of the rock would affect the rope and how it tugged on the pieces. I also failed to realize how small the range is for a small cam as the Metolius 1. As a result of these mistakes, I believe they are what caused my pieces to pull.

I learned three very valuable lessons. In the future, I will always use slings with my nuts and extend them if there is any bulge in the rock or if I am close the ground. I will also remember how small the range is on the small cams and be sure not to under-cam them. I will also really set my nuts when placing them and make sure they are sitting securely in the cracks. (Source: Edited from a report submitted by Lisa Wang)

(Editor's Note: We always appreciate it when climbers submit their own reports and self-analysis.)

FALLS ON ROCK (17), PROTECTION PULLED OUT (7), INADEQUATE PROTECTION (4), BELAY ERRORS (4), RAPPEL ERROR
New York, Mohonk Preserve, Shawangunks

Twenty reports were submitted for 2010 (including the narrative above).

There were three 40-foot falls, one 50-foot fall, and one 80-foot fall. The latter was due to a miscommunication between the belayer and the climber.

The average age of the climbers was 36 and the level of route difficulty was 5.8. The injuries included three fractures, eight sprains/strains, three lacerations, two dislocations, and one crushed finger. One of the dislocations occurred when a 57 year old just lifted his foot while climbing on a self-belay top-rope. It re-located, but he had to be transported to his vehicle.

Ten climbers were inexperienced, eight were experienced, and the others were unknown. (Source: From reports submitted by Mohonk Preserve)

FALL ON ROCK, PLACED INADEQUATE PROTECTION
North Carolina, Stone Mountain State Park

On February 27, my two partners and I were getting ready to climb Mercury's Lead off the tree ledge. Two young women (I'll call them Jane and Joan) came walking down from the far end of the tree ledge and said they planned to lead the Great Arch (5.5). We chatted for a little bit and while Joan was racking up for her lead, our leader started off on Mercury's with me belaying. He got to the first bolt and was scoping out the rock above. Since he was in a secure spot, I felt comfortable glancing over to see how things were going on the Arch.

Joan had placed a piece of pro (a medium cam) about ten feet up and was climbing above it into the section where the crack widens before turning the first corner, approximately 20 feet up on the route. She was making a series of layback moves and when she got up to the corner, her hands came off. At this point, she was far enough above her single placement that it never came into play stopping her fall. She skidded down the face for several feet when it appeared that one or both feet caught on something causing her to flip backwards. She free fell the remaining distance to the ground (8–10 feet) and landed flat on her back.

Because I had my partner on belay, I couldn't respond immediately, but the third person in our group and Jane (Joan's belayer) went to check her condition. She remained motionless on her back. I could tell from where I was standing that she was conscious and that her eyes were moving.

My partner replaced his draw with a "bail-out 'biner" on the first bolt and I lowered him so we could assist. By that time, Joan was sitting up and moving her arms around and talking. She reported pain in her arms, hands, and legs, but didn't show any signs of broken bones. She also said she'd hit her head (she was wearing a helmet) and that she had a mild headache. This immediately sent up red flags to me for head trauma, so I asked her if she was feeling dizzy or experiencing any visual distortion. She said she wasn't.

The landing zone was fortunately free of rocks, but there were numerous tree roots surrounding the area where Joan landed. When she came to rest after the fall, it looked like her head was resting on a root, so presumably this was the point of impact for the head-blow she reported. Her arms showed obvious bruises where she rolled up her sleeves and there was redness on her hands, probably from scraping on the rock. Cursory examination of her scalp showed no broken skin or bleeding. Before long, she was up and moving around, flexing her arms and legs and rotating her head from side to side to see what hurt and what didn't. She also expressed embarrassment about having taken a fall from what she saw as an easy climb.

Jane and Joan had come up to the tree ledge with just one rope; they told us their intention was to climb the Arch and then descend by the walk-off trail. With that no longer an option, they would need to rappel to get to the ground, which of course is a two-rope rappel. We decided to fix their rope from the U-Slot rap station so they could do a single-line rappel, then drop their rope to them. Jane went first with their gear so she'd be on hand for a fireman's belay if necessary, then Joan rigged her belay/rappel device and rapped down. Before they left, we urged that Joan get medical attention as some head injuries that seem minor can turn out to be life-threatening. They assured us they would do that, and that was the last we saw of them.

Analysis

In terms of observations and analysis of this accident, I guess my two main points would be: One, know your limits; and two, place adequate protection. The Great Arch isn't a highly difficult route, but the start in my experience has the hardest moves on the whole climb. Getting up and around that first corner involves some lay-back moves that are fairly strenuous. The leader in question seemed to be struggling with the lay-back. Her feet didn't seem to be high enough when she was making the moves. She would benefit from working similar moves on a top-rope until she gets more strength, technique, and confidence. As to protection, the problem this leader had was that she was so far above the only piece she had placed that it couldn't protect her fall. Before making the hard lay-back moves, it would have been good to have placed another piece of pro. No one likes to carry a big rack at Stone Mountain, but if you're not strong enough to make the opening moves without protection, bring the gear you need. One positive comment is that the leader was wearing a helmet. If she hadn't been, the blow to her head when she hit the root could have been more serious. (Source: Edited from a report by John Liles, witness)

ICE COLLAPSED, FALL ON ICE, CLIMBING ALONE AND UNROPED
North Carolina, Blue Ridge Parkway, Doughton Park

The body of Ralph Fickle (59), an experienced climber and guide, was found on March 4 about 200 feet below the Blue Ridge Parkway, a half-mile south of the Bluffs Restaurant at Doughton Park. Apparently, Ralph was free-soloing Farmer's Daughter. It seems that about 90 feet up and 10 feet from where the climb backs off and the lower angle ice tops out, the free hanging curtain of ice he was on completely fractured. Ralph had rigged a top anchored bail out line in case he felt the need to retreat. His ATC was clipped to the belay loop of his harness. Due to the large section of ice that broke, he did not have time to retrieve the line.

Ralph fell to the base of the climb and slid down slope. He suffered head trauma and did not pass instantly, but soon after coming to a stop, as evidenced by the fact that he had time to remove gloves and touch the wound, but not much after that.

Analysis

Solo climbing and late season ice don't mix, especially in the Southeast. (Source: Josh McMann, from a post on carolinaclimbers.org)

FALL ON ROCK, POORLY CONSTRUCTED ANCHOR
North Carolina, Hanging Rock State Park, Moore's Wall

On May 2, Drew Witt (28) and I, Lee Kennedy (23) were climbing Zoo View (5.7+). I set up the belay by building an anchor on the large boulder located on the Crow's Nest (Pitch 1, < 80 feet). Before Drew started the second pitch, I decided to make the anchor redundant by slinging a smaller boulder located under the larger primary boulder. Drew started the pitch and climbed about 30 feet, placed a cam (unknown #), climbed an additional ten feet, then fell.

I was yanked directly to the left, which loaded the smaller boulder, dislodging it. It would have fallen, but I had it slung tight enough that it stayed attached, hanging below me! It was heavy enough (maybe a couple of hundred pounds) that it prevented me from moving. Luckily, there was someone else on the Crow's Nest who helped me pull the boulder to a small ledge where we were able to pull the sling off, then trundled the boulder to the ground.

Analysis

I was inexperienced holding trad falls and was unaware of the forces involved. Most importantly, I should have checked the secondary boulder to make sure it was adequate for an anchor. This can be done in a number of ways. Do a hug test—any boulder you can get your arms around is too small to use as an anchor. Boulders used for anchors should be secured to the surrounding environment and should not move when tested. Rule out any boulder that appears ready to be tipped over the edge. In hindsight, the large boulder would have been an adequate anchor by itself. (Source: Lee Kennedy)

FALL ON ROCK, RAPPEL FAILURE/ERROR, INADEQUATE EQUIPMENT
North Carolina, Paint Rock

Paint rock (also known as Graffiti Rock), a popular roadside rappelling and training site in Pisgah National Forest was the scene of a rappelling accident on August 15 involving Jane and John Doe.

John had limited climbing experience through the military; his girlfriend Jane had no climbing experience. The pair had two ropes, one a climbing rope, the other a non-climbing rope purchased from a box store (origin or type unknown). Both ropes were anchored for a rappel.

Both climbers were wearing climbing harnesses. Jane was attached to the box store rope with a prusik loop. The prusik was constructed out of a "shoe lace" looking cord (i.e. not designed for climbing) and attached to her harness with a carabiner. She was not using a belay/rappel device. John was attached to the second rappel rope with the rope running through a carabiner attached to his harness. He had no belay/rappel device.

The couple moved to the edge of the cliff to begin their rappel with their backs to the fall line. Based on an examination of the scene, it appeared that Jane fell first while "rappelling" and landed on a four-foot wide rock shelf approximately 40 feet from the top and 15–20 feet from the ground. John went down to help her and then fell to the ground about 60 feet below.

Both climbers were discovered with burns on their hands. John suffered two leg fractures (one an open fracture) and Jane had a broken wrist and a spinal injury.

Analysis

This accident speaks for itself. Both individuals had no business attempting to rappel with no knowledge, inadequate equipment, and experience. Upon inspection, Jane's "prusik" along with the sheath of her rope melted, causing her to lose control. Chances are if she had let go of the prusik sooner it may have prevented her from serious injury. John never had a chance. His burns were a result of his hand being the sole friction device on the rope. He may have forgotten to wrap the spine of his carabiner to create a carabiner wrap (common in military rappelling) in his haste to aid Jane. Rappelling presents a unique set of dangers that aren't found in other forms of climbing. A functional belay rappel device, a backup system utilizing an autoblock or similar friction knot and the knowledge on how to use it along with the proper equipment may have prevented this unfortunate incident. (Source: K. Delap and A. Attarian)

FALL ON ROCK, OFF-ROUTE
North Carolina, Blue Ridge Parkway, Shiprock

The three of us had been climbing since late morning on September 4. It was now early evening and two of us decided to try an unnamed route described to us by a climber we met on our previous trip to Ship Rock. We checked out the features and picked out the route as best we could from the ground. I geared up and began climbing. The first part of the climb involved a juggy, run-out section up some blocks and over a small bulge to the base of a low angle slab. The slab offered plenty of protection, so I geared up for the roof above me. After placing good gear near the lip of the roof, I pulled over it without much difficulty and placed what would be my final piece, a

BD #2 nut, in a bottleneck six feet or so above the roof.

At this point the climb thinned out into a featureless face route for the remaining 15 to 20 feet of the climb. From the beta I had on the route, I knew to the left of my route was a route a grade harder and to the right was a route two grades harder, so I figured the path of least resistance was the route I was on. I continued up and slightly to the left where I saw the most features. As I continued up, more features became apparent on the rock, and after climbing through the majority of the blank face, I came to realize I had split off onto the route to my left, a full grade harder and more run-out than my anticipated route. I stayed calm and took a quick look around, eyeing what looked like a fairly deep three-finger pocket at the very edge of my reach that, if I could get a hold of, would get me through the run-out section to good protection above me. Realizing I had no other options, I committed to the hold hoping for the best. The hold was much shallower and more sloped than anticipated—not enough for my pumped out fingers to clinch onto.

The first 12–15 feet of the fall was air. I began to think everything was going to end smoothly until I realized I was passing my last piece. Remembering the low angle slab below me, I braced for impact. Initially I landed square on my right heel, then fell sideways and onto my left side.

After explaining what I did wrong and how I got off route to my partner, I sat down near the base of the climb for a while until my partner led the correct pitch and cleaned the gear. With their help, I limped down the short approach trail to the Blue Ridge Parkway and waited by the side of the road for my ride. The damage: a fractured heel bone, a cracked rib, and plenty of scrapes and bruises, but I live to climb another day.

Analysis

Always climb within your limits and, though I didn't hit my head, wear a helmet! (Source: Will Chirico)

FALL ON ROCK, ROPE PULLS THROUGH BELAY DEVICE
North Carolina, Hawksbill Mountain, Linville Gorge Wilderness

On September 20, AG (26) and AA (30) were climbing at the "Fischesser Wall,"a little known sport climbing area on the upper wall of Hawksbill Mountain located on the eastside of the Linville Gorge Wilderness. AG was leading a 5.8+ climb with AA belaying. They were using a 60-meter rope and were both wearing helmets. The topo of the climbing area notes the climb is 100 feet long, making a 60-meter rope adequate. AG climbed it clean and was being lowered by AA. AG was cleaning the bolt closest to the ground and asked AA how much rope she had left. He replied it was fine. At 2:45 p.m., just after AG cleaned the last piece of gear, AG was lowered off the end of the rope and fell to the ground.

The bolt was about 25–30 feet off the ground. She and eyewitnesses (BG and CM) believe the fall was 15–20 feet. She landed on her tailbone and rolled backwards five feet down a small slope on to her left side. She complained of pain in her lower back, buttocks, and left hip. She tried to stand and immediately felt nauseous and that her legs couldn't support her. It became clear to her climbing partners that she would not be able to walk out.

At 3:03 p.m., CM called the North Carolina Outward Bound School (NCOBS) to report the incident. NCOBS sent a total of 15 staff to assist in the carry-out. Burke County Rescue arrived with one Paramedic and three volunteers just as OB staff were completing the packaging of AG in the litter. In the field, paramedics started an IV for fluids and gave AG a total of six mg of morphine over a two-hour period. Initial evaluation suggested severe bruising and abrasions, but no spinal damage or fractures. Later, AG was informed that a piece of small bone at the bottom of the sacrum was broken.

Analysis

The 60-meter rope in use belonged to BG, who had climbed the same route using the same rope on a number of previous occasions without incident. The position of the belayer in relationship to the route (uphill or downhill) may have played a role in the length of the rope, in this case shortening it by 20 feet. To prevent incidents like this from happening, belayers need to get into the habit of tying into the end of the rope and either placing a knot at the end of the rope or securing the end of the rope. (Source: Edited from a report by Julie Springsteen, NCOBS)

FALL ON ROCK, ARM LACERATED BY CARABINER
North Carolina, Pilot Mountain State Park

On September 25, Bennet Harris (30) and Tom Drewes (34) were climbing Arms Control (5.11c). Tom was about to pull the final roof. I was watching him climb extremely closely as I intended to climb the route and wanted to see what he did.

He placed a 48-inch sling on the last bolt he clipped at the roof and a 24-inch sling combined with a quick draw to extend it on his second-to-last bolt. Because he had climbed past a smaller roof, a lead fall should have put him in the air. I watched him lean out to grab the jug beyond the big roof. His hand looked a little shaky as he reached for the hold, leaning far back from his stance under the roof. I remember thinking, "If he's having trouble reaching for that, I'm really going to be in trouble."

At this point he fell, and stopped about eight to ten feet below where he started, in mid-air. (Four feet of this was due to the sling). It did not look like a bad fall; it looked safe and his belayer caught the fall with no problem.

It was about a full second before he yelled and we saw him looking at his forearm, which had been sliced open to the bones from mid-forearm to the palm, causing him to bleed profusely! We lowered him and called 911 within seconds. A first responder, a surgeon in residency, and a doctor were all climbing near-by and gave assistance until he was carried out.

Analysis

At first we couldn't figure anything out. Did he hit a rock during his fall? The features below were smooth and sloped and he fell into mid-air. Could he have run his arm over a bolt? The bolts weren't anywhere near his body during the fall because his arm was way out reaching over a roof.

I had seen a story about a Colorado climber becoming impaled on a carabiner at the elbow about a month ago. Because of this, I wondered if catching his arm on the carabiner might have been the cause. It seemed unlikely, since I'd never heard of it happening until I saw the picture a month before, but there was no other equipment or rock near him. I climbed Arms Control up to the point where the long draws were used (his last clipped bolts) to clean as much of his gear for him as I could. I decided to leave the last two slings and carabiners to lower from, and did get all the way to them so I could examine them. During my exam, I noted the quickdraw carabiner on the second-to-last clip was clean. The Helium carabiner on the 48-inch sling had blood and other evidence on it of entering a human! There was no blood above this and actually very little below, for about 15 feet, since he didn't really start bleeding until he was being lowered. I am certain this carabiner was the one that entered his arm and ripped it from forearm to palm. (Source: Anne McLaughlin, witness)

STRANDED, ROPE STUCK
North Carolina, The Amphitheater, Linville Gorge Wilderness Area

Two climbers with limited experience on moderate trad routes planned on spending several days camping and climbing at Linville Gorge. On November 23, they hiked in and began climbing Good Heavens (5.4), located in the Amphitheater. Their goal was to climb something "easy" in order to become familiar with the rock in the area. They were climbing on a 70-meter rope.

Halfway into the approximately 500-foot climb, the leader (L) disappeared around a corner. Eventually the rope stopped moving. At this point the belayer (B) tried to communicate with L to identify the problem and discovered that because of his position and the overhanging rock he was unable to communicate. B began tugging on the rope and noted that the rope was stuck. He waited for an hour, trying to get a response from L with no success. B didn't know if L was injured. L was without food, water, or his jacket, since they were left for B to carry. B anchored his rope and rappelled down the tail of his rope as far as he could, then down-climbed approximately 30 feet.

On his way out for help, he was able to call out at approximately 4:50 p.m. to initiate a rescue. Climbers in the area and rescue personnel gathered and divided into two teams. One team would hike to the base of the climb and begin climbing to L, while the other team would hike to the top.

Operations let everyone know via radio communication that a National Guard Blackhawk helicopter with rescuers was enroute to assist. It arrived and located L at 10:02 p.m. and reported that he was in good condition. L was in the helicopter by 10:58 p.m., about six hours after his partner called for help. The helicopter also picked-off the two climbers who were on the route to assist. (Source: Edited from a post by Mike Broome, carolinaclimbers.org, and www2.morganton.com/news

Analysis

Climbing in Linville Gorge should not be taken lightly, even when attempting easy to moderate routes. It is one of the few wilderness areas in the East that offers high quality climbing experiences at all levels in a remote setting. Access is limited and demanding. For this reason climbers should be self-reliant and have the appropriate technical and self-rescue skills to initiate a self-rescue if possible. (Source: Aram Attarian)

FALL ON SNOW/ICE, SKI MOUNTAINEERING
Oregon, Mount Hood

On June 15, while ski traversing the Coe glacier at about the 9500-foot elevation, Robert Wiebe (58) went out ahead of his two companions and apparently slipped during a turn. Another party of four Hood River Crag Rats saw him fall about 700 feet. They notified authorities and skied down to assist.

Wiebe died from his injuries before a Blackhawk helicopter from Salem could reach their scene.

Analysis

Late season glacier skiing often involves exposed glacier, ice, and rock. Ski mountaineers should be adept and equipped for self-arrest when on or above steep slopes or crevasses. When traversing technical sections, skiers should be prepared to remove skis and use crampons, ice axes, and rope as the terrain and experience level dictate.

FALL ON ROCK AND SNOW, INEXPERIENCE, INADEQUATE EQUIPMENT AND CLOTHING, CLIMBING ALONE
Oregon, Mount Thielsen

On June 25, Tristan Massie (40), visiting Oregon from Maryland, was free-solo climbing the spectacular talus of the class four summit of Mount Thielsen when he slipped, fell about 20 feet on volcanic blocks, and then slid about 50 feet on the steep snow field below the summit.

Tristan lay on the snow with painful and disabling injuries, unable to move more than a few feet, for the remainder of the day on Friday, when he heard a climber crossing the remote snowfield late in the afternoon. He was just barely able to attract the climber's attention.

He had left his cell phone in his summit pack, stashed near his hiking boots at the foot of his proposed rock climb to the summit. The lone climber, Stewart Slay, had a cell phone and called 911 for Search and Rescue assistance at 5:07 p.m. Tristan was lying lightly clad, directly on the snow, under the threat of frost bite and hypothermia. Time passed and it grew very cold and dark before the Douglas County Sheriff's Search and Rescue team could be mobilized and climb the snow covered slopes to the two climbers at 12:30 a.m. During the night, Tristan was lowered on a stretcher, down the steep snow and scree slope northwest of the summit to easier ground, where, at 10 a.m. Saturday, he was hoisted up into an Oregon National Guard helicopter and flown to St. Charles Hospital in Bend, Oregon.

Analysis

Experience tells us to climb new summits with known companions. From Maryland, Tristan Massie had scheduled a guided climb of some Cascades peaks near Bend, but remaining snow fields had put the peaks out of reasonable reach for the guided group. Mount Thielsen was suggested as an easy peak. He is a strong long-distance runner. He reached the summit blocks in just four hours from the trailhead, despite drifts of snow on the trail and the large snowfield below the summit. Local experience tells us that few people climb Mount Thielsen this early in the summer.

Tammy Massie notes that Tristan did not carry his cell phone in his pants pocket or their SPOT-2 "GPS satellite communicator" and that he did not have a topo map of Mount Thielsen. He did not have a helmet, usually used when climbing peaks in the volcanic Oregon Cascades. Rather than carrying his small summit pack on the scramble, he had left it at the base of the rock face. He was unable to reach his summit pack and phone or his larger pack, which, however, did not have gear for a stranding overnight in the forecast conditions. He might not have survived the night, lying lightly dressed on the snow in sub-zero temperatures and summit winds, without his chance encounter.

We have confirmed that Tristan had not set a specific time for a designated Responsible Person to call 911 in the event that he did not check in or answer his cell phone. Tammie Massie states: "Unfortunately in the case of Tristan's adventure in OR I would only have called 911 on Sunday night when he did not get back on his flight." (Source: Robert Speik)

FALL ON SNOW, UNABLE TO SELF-ARREST
Oregon, Mount Hood, Southside

While descending the Mazama Chute variation of the Southside route at 7:00 a.m. on July 7, Bryan Call (25) lost his footing and fell about 200 feet because he was unable to self-arrest. His slide ended at the Hot Rocks area. He had multiple abrasions, a sore elbow, and a knee injury.

Nearby climbers rendered first aid and notified authorities by cell phone. Call was evacuated by a ground team manned by Portland Mountain Rescue, American Medical Response, and the Timberline Ski Patrol.

Analysis
Self-arrest is a basic skill that must be mastered by all climbers. The steepness and exposure on this route resulted in at least two other injury accidents in the same month. (Source: Jeff Scheetz, Portland Mountain Rescue)

FALL ON ROCK, COLD FINGERS
Oregon, French's Dome
On September 4, Joe Leineweber (29) was leading a 5.8 to 5.9 bolted route on French's Dome. The weather was somewhat damp and there were wet places on the rock. Leineweber was reaching for a bolt when he fell about 20–30 feet. During the fall his right foot hit a projecting ledge, causing him a serious fracture of his tibia and fibula.

His climbing partner and a bystander lowered him to the ground. The climbing partner drove to cell phone coverage to call for an ambulance. Meanwhile three climbers (including two Portland Mountain Rescue members) backed of a nearby route to provide care until the ambulance arrived. Leineweber was carried to the ambulance by firefighters, ambulance crew, PMR members and other climbers.

Analysis
The slip was probably a result of the cold's affect on his fingers' ability to perceive variation in the rock. In the Leineweber's opinion, wet rock was not a factor. (Source: From a report by Hal Lilywhite, Portland Mountain Rescue, and Joe Forrester)

BELAYER ERROR - LEADER PULLED OFF, FALL ON ROCK CLIMB
Utah, American Fork Canyon
On August 10, two experienced climbers climbing together for the first time met at the mouth of American Fork Canyon at the suggestion of the younger climber, Christian Burrell (25), who proposed establishing a new route. James Garrett (59) had established many first ascents traditionally from the ground up, whereas Burrell, though he had been active establishing new routes, had confined his style to top down methods. He seemed eager to learn to drill on lead from the more traditional Garrett and had proposed a moderate-appearing slab where he had looked at doing a new route. Burrell also seemed convinced the climbing would be no harder than 5.6 to 5.7, a climbing grade somewhat lacking in American Fork Canyon. The first pitch (5.10ish) went well, though patches of loose scree intermingled with

the compact rock and belays were established to protect the belayer from inevitable rockfall. (Both climbers wore helmets.)

Burrell decided to jumar instead of seconding or climbing on top-rope to follow the first pitch. While leading the second pitch (the limestone accepted gear poorly), four bolts were drilled on lead. After the fourth bolt, the angle decreased considerably onto a loose scree slope. Garrett was now about 25 meters above Burrell, and after passing a small corner, visual and verbal contact became limited. Canyon river and car traffic noise further complicated communication. Burrell reported some rockfall, but Garrett suddenly felt a huge amount of drag on the rope as he climbed easy, albeit loose, terrain about two meters above the last bolt he had placed. He struggled with maintaining his position on the slope, but inevitably sent down more loose rocks in scrambling to maintain his position and avoid falling down the slab. No rock fall came from above. Suddenly and without warning, Burrell put his entire body into pulling the rope in as if he had someone on a top-rope who was falling or had yelled, "Take!" Only this was not the case.

As Garrett started to fall, he tried consciously to relax his body to lessen the injuries knowing that his last protection bolt was not far below. Instead, he fell and tumbled more than 20 meters, finally coming to a stop a mere three to four meters above the belayer. Garrett's helmet was so deformed that it fell off his head at the end of the fall and tumbled to the belay ledge.

Garrett, an RN and former Flight Nurse, self-diagnosed his most life threatening injuries and concerned about airway issues, asked the belayer to lower him the short distance to the belay ledge where Burrell could be free to better assess/care/and address the ABC's and comfort Garrett. Burrell decided to call 911 first and then followed their instructions not to move Garrett further and simply wait for EMS Rescue Helicopter evacuation.

After about 45 minutes, rescue crews reached Garrett by ground. They were instructed by Garrett how to install another bolt next to the second one placed while on lead. This provided a two-bolt anchor from which Garrett could be lowered by litter the short distance to the ledge. On the belay ledge, a backboard was placed and an IV with LR was started to allow the administration of pain medication. Garrett complained of mostly right chest wall pain. Thirty minutes later, Garrett was hoisted out by an Air Ambulance helicopter and flown to the hospital where X-rays revealed fifteen broken bones in the C-Spine, T-Spine, right hand, right ribs, and right foot. A right pneumothorax and lung contusion added to the list of injuries. No paralysis or head injury was incurred, but fusion of the T-spine was later necessary. The Black Diamond Helmet that absorbed all of the head blows clearly saved a life on this day.

Analysis

It is really difficult to deduce what exactly was going through Burrell's mind. Tension should never be applied to the lead rope when the leader is clearly above his last piece of protection. Though he had climbed for many years and rap-drilled numerous new routes, Burrell appeared new to the idea of traditional climbing and bolt installation as one ascends. He also possibly confused a falling loose stone for a falling climber. For the leader to have to endure such a long and painful fall when he was really so close to his last piece implies that the belayer additionally most likely lost control of the rope as well.

Burrell chose never to discuss the incident with Garrett. It can only be assumed that he realized his mistake after he had applied such massive amounts of tension. He then either fed out more rope to "overcorrect" his initial error or compounded the mistake by loosing control of the belay.

As Burrell suggested the project from the beginning would be a slab climb no harder than 5.7 in difficulty, Garrett should probably have decided to abandon the project from the two-bolt belay anchor he had installed after completing the first loose 5.10 pitch. In hindsight, this would certainly have prevented the mishap that followed while leading the second pitch. Despite the looseness or chossy characteristics of the climbing, Garrett never felt outside of his comfort zone so had independently decided to continue. Perhaps mutual trust between climbing partners must be built up over time.

Also, while cell phones are good to have for use in the case of an emergency, many young climbers seem to be stuck in a nether land between the virtual and real worlds. Some younger belayers may not be fully aware of the consequences of multi-tasking. The importance of the relationship between a focused and competent belayer to a safe ascent/climb cannot be overstated. (Source: James Garrett)

(Additional comment: The implication that Burrell was using his cell phone while belaying is disturbing to say the least. This editor has written a piece called "Climbing With Blind Dates." It indicates some of the discussion points to engage in before setting out with someone whose climbing experience is known only through conversation. Source: Jed Williamson)

BELAY AND TIE-IN ERROR, FALL ON ROCK, NO HARD HAT
Utah, Big Cottonwood Canyon, Dogwood Crag

On September 26, University of Utah, Remote Rescue Training's High-Angle Rescue Technician class was practicing rope rescue systems at the Dogwood crag in Big Cottonwood Canyon when a nearby climber, not associated with the class, fell approximately 80 feet to the ground. The class immediately stopped the scenario and switched in to "real" rescue mode. The lead instructor delegated two students to stay at the top of the cliff where cell phone coverage is more reliable and call 911 to initiate the Emergency Medical System. A hasty team with two instructors and two students (all EMT's) were immediately dispatched to the base of the cliff where the fallen climber landed. Two students went to the road to help direct EMS personnel to the patient more efficiently. The remaining students and instructor packed up all equipment that seemed likely to be helpful, including medical equipment and the stokes litter and went down to the base of the cliff, on standby to assist as needed.

The hasty team arrived at the patient approximately three minutes after the fall. The patient, Jeremy (22), was sitting up with his hands clenched to his chest. The hasty team leader and Remote Rescue Training instructor, Nate Ostis, completed a full patient assessment. Due to the mechanism of injury, spinal precautions were maintained. EMS arrived on scene approximately ten minutes after the fall. The litter evacuation was non-technical and took approximately two minutes.

We know a few facts about how the fall occurred, gathered from our observations and interviews. Jeremy was top-roping with his rope fed directly through the anchor chains. Rather than tying into the end of the rope with a figure-8 follow through, he had tied a figure-8 on a bight and clipped the bight into his harness with a locking carabiner. When he neared the top of the climb (approximately 80 feet from the ground), he leaned back expecting to be lowered by his belayer to the ground. At that moment his attachment to the knot failed, because for some reason the carabiner gate "hyper-extended" and the bight of the knot came free from the carabiner. Realizing the dire situation he was in, Jeremy reached out and grabbed the only thing he could—the strand of rope between the belayer and the anchor. Initially there was no counter balance on the rope and Jeremy continued to free fall, but after a few feet, the knot at the end of the rope wedged up against the chains, essentially fixing the single strand of rope so that he was able to slow his descent and keep himself upright by gripping the rope. Approximately 15 feet from the ground, he hit and broke through a tree, which further slowed his descent.

The rescue team was unable to contact the fallen climber after turning care over to EMS but news reports said that the climber was released the next day with "minor injuries."

Analysis

Tying into the end of the rope has long been the standard practice for this type of situation and would have avoided this accident all together. In situations where clipping into the rope makes more sense, many people would make the case for two locking carabiners at the attachment point. We do not know whether Jeremy was clipped in to the belay loop or the harness itself.

There are a few hypotheses of what may have happened. First, it seems very likely that the carabiner was not locked when Jeremy leaned back on the rope. Second, perhaps the carabiner was not even closed entirely, having been caught on either some fabric of the harness, the rope, or on the locking mechanism itself. Third, after not being closed, the carabiner may have been somehow loaded along the major axis and then, after it was stretched out, loaded along the minor axis. A fourth possibility is that the carabiner may have been pushed open and loaded to the side in such a way that the gate could swing around the side of the nose, allowing it to hyperextend. Other options are certainly possible.

Jeremy was not wearing a helmet. Although many people do not wear helmets when top-roping at single pitch crags such as this, he was extremely lucky to survive an 80-foot fall without sustaining any head injuries.

Passing the belay/lowering rope through the chains is often considered poor etiquette because it puts substantial wear on the chains as person after person lowers off the route. In this situation, had the knot jammed up against a couple of carabiners, it may or may not have held the force that the knot jammed against the small links was able to hold. Strangely, having the rope pass through the chains may have helped save Jeremy's life. (Source: Andy Rich)

SLIP ON ROCK, RAPPEL ERROR – POOR TECHNIQUE, INADEQUATE INSTRUCTION AND SUPERVISION
Virginia, Hidden Rocks

On September 11, guides were managing a rappel at the top of the route Snowblower. A climber became nervous stepping over the edge, slipped to the left of observers, spun several times, and struck her head on the rock.

Guides responded by activating a rescue beacon and rappelling to the unconscious climber to render aid. A cervical collar was improvised to stabilize her head and a 3:1 pulley system was constructed after determining that raising her was the most suitable approach.

The climber became pain responsive within five minutes and verbally responsive within ten minutes. After being stabilized at the top of the cliff, EMS arrived shortly after to carry her out. The patient had no TBI (traumatic brain injury), but did have a laceration on the back of the head and shoulder a injury.

Analysis

Prior to introducing students or clients to a long or committing rappel, the basics of rappelling should be introduced or reviewed on the ground, a low angle slab, or on a less demanding rappel, and demonstrated by a responsible guide or instructor. This approach allows the individual being taught a better understanding of the techniques and fundamentals of the task at hand. (Source: From a September 14 post on www.rockclimbing.com)

CORNICE COLLAPSE – FALL ON SNOW
Washington, Mount St. Helens

On February 15, Joseph Bohlig (52) from Kelso fell into the crater at about 1:00 p.m. A veteran climber on his 69th trek up the mountain, Bohlig was posing for a picture about five feet from the crater's edge when the snow beneath him collapsed.

His longtime climbing partner and best friend, Scott Salkovics, watched in horror as Bohlig slid about 1,500 feet along rock and ice and settled into the crater wall at a 70-degree angle. "He was just getting his picture taken, and all of the sudden I saw a crack and him grasping for the edge and a look of surprise and fear on his face," said Salkovics (49) of Longview. "And then he disappeared."

The pair reached the summit in four hours, Salkovics said. After taking off his backpack and jacket and handing a camera to another hiker, Bohlig was backing up toward the edge of the crater when the snow gave way, Salkovics said. The hiker with the camera threw himself toward the edge but was unable to catch Bohlig. "The first thing I did was start screaming, 'No, no!'" Salkovics said. "It was the hugest sense of helplessness I've ever had."

Salkovics said he tossed a backpack with supplies into the crater in hopes it would help his friend. It was determined later the backpack had landed out of Bohlig's reach.

A helicopter from Whidbey Island Naval Air Station removed Bohlig's body from the south crater wall at 2:45 p.m. It was the fourth attempt to reach Bohlig after weather halted two tries Monday and one Tuesday morning.

Analysis

Climbing accidents are rare but not unprecedented on Mount St. Helens. There hasn't been a climbing death on the mountain since the 1970s, Skamania County Sheriff David Brown said.

Richard Bohlig said he hopes his son's death will serve as a reminder to other climbers. "I hope that they would learn to don't be so sure of the edge of the rim," he said. "It can break off almost any time, and that's what happened."

Dave Cox, Skamania County Undersheriff, said he wasn't sure whether the death would have any impact on safety procedures on the mountain. "I just think we're dealing with a very unfortunate accident today," he said. (Source: Edited from an article by Brian Rosenthal in the *Seattle Times*)

FALL INTO CREVASSE, WEATHER – WHITEOUT CONDITIONS AND HIGH WINDS, OFF ROUTE, INEXPERIENCE
Washington, Mount Rainier, Camp Muir

On April 27, park climbing rangers, assisted by guides from International Mountain Guides and Alpine Ascents International, successfully rescued two Canadian climbers, Simon Brunet (23) and Genivive Morund (early

20's), who had fallen into a crevasse by walking off a cornice during whiteout conditions. She indicated that they were in the vicinity of Camp Muir, having traveled over the Muir Snowfield and past Anvil Rock prior to falling into a crevasse or over a cliff for a distance of 50 meters. She indicated that her climbing partner was unconscious at that time (Monday afternoon). She was unable to provide a location, and early indications were that one of the two was badly injured.

Rangers began making their way to Camp Muir to stage for early morning search operations. Weather conditions on the mountain were adverse, with sustained 70 mph winds gusting up to 90 mph and temperatures down to 23 degrees. A helicopter was placed on standby for morning operations. Early on Tuesday morning, Morund made contact with the park on her cell phone. Questioning by park officials provided critical information that led to identifying their location in the area just below Camp Muir. The rangers were able to locate and extract the two climbers using high angle rescue gear. Both climbers suffered from relatively minor injuries and hypothermia. As they had fallen into the crevasse with their packs on, the two were able to set their tent up, get into their sleeping bags, and even heat up soup. However, the intensity of the storm required them to continuously shovel snow off their tent throughout the night to prevent it from collapsing. An MD 530 helicopter was used to fly the climbers off the mountain.

They were transported to Morton Hospital and subsequently released at 2100. Ranger Glenn Kessler was IC on this operation. (Source: Edited from a report by Chuck Young, Chief Ranger)

Analysis

The climbers fell when they were navigating in very windy whiteout conditions. They said they were following a wanded route when they fell, but in actuality they had failed to make a crucial heading change around 9,200 feet and had wandered off route in a dangerous area. This spot on the Muir Snowfield is an area with no visual reference. They had left for Camp Muir in a storm with stormier weather forecast.

Major contributing factors were a combination of inexperience, severe winter weather, and poor communication. These two were experienced sport climbers but had not spent any significant time in alpine environments. They had overestimated their ability to deal with a harsh winter environment in glaciated terrain. They had no heavy insulating layers when they were found. Brunet and Morund set up their tent on a steep slope underneath the cornice from which they had fallen. The slope was receiving huge amounts of wind-transported snow, but they were unable or unwilling to move out of this very dangerous spot. Therefore, their sleeping bags, stoves and every other piece of equipment were useless because they were thoroughly soaked and frozen. (Source: Edited from a report by Cooper Self, Climbing Ranger)

SEVERE WEATHER – FROSTBITE, HYPOTHERMIA, COMMUNICATION PROBLEMS
Washington, Mount Rainier, Ingraham Glacier

On the evening of May 20, a report came into Camp Muir describing a bad scene in which a guided team of twelve (four guides and eight clients) and another group of four guides (different company) were pinned down on the Ingraham Glacier in extremely severe weather. The groups were descending late from a summit climb, while the four guides had gone to dismantle a camp at Ingraham Flats due to the harsh forecast. The weather had gone from rather pleasant in the morning hours to a full on winter storm by 1500, complete with lots of snow, temperatures in the single digits, and winds that averaged 90 mph with top speeds in excess of 110 mph at Camp Muir. Visibility was very bad. The group of four guides with no clients was able to crawl their way back into Muir and relay pertinent info to Climbing Ranger Cooper Self, who was the only NPS employee at Muir at the time. Communication was very difficult between groups in camp and non-existent with the guided teams still on the mountain.

A plan was put together to send a team of four "fresh" guides across the Cowlitz Glacier, staying on route in an effort to look for and assist the unaccounted for teams of guides and clients still on the mountain. During this time, one roped team found its way into the camp of clients, where one client showed signs of severe hypothermia. Efforts began to re-warm this individual in one of the guide service weather ports. The search team of four was forced to turn back only minutes out of Camp Muir due to the extreme conditions. They regrouped and remained on standby should conditions improve at all. Over the next few hours, the rest of the guided teams found their way into Muir. Many of the clients were extremely fatigued and cold, but none had any major medical issues. Two of the guides sustained partial to full thickness frostbite to skin on their fingers and faces. By 2245, everyone was accounted for and safely inside some building, where they all waited inside for the weather to get better. The next day during improved conditions, all involved persons were able to walk themselves off the mountain and get to definitive medical care as needed.

Analysis

Although the storm that was encountered that day was unusual in its severity, it had been forecast. For some reason, this forecast was not relayed with enough urgency to the guided groups, who were subsequently caught in it late in the day. The storm did not hit really hard until between 1300–1400, a time when guided climbs are usually already off the route. The NPS was not contacted right away due to the incorrect thinking that no rangers were at camp.

Had better communication happened, the guide service would not have been out so late on the upper mountain. Search efforts and organization of resources could have been expedited if the NPS had been contacted earlier. It is hard to say if earlier search efforts would have been productive in getting the guided group back into camp earlier and with fewer injuries, but searching in daylight would have been easier than searching in the dark. When the NPS was contacted (about three hours after the first signs of problems), no one knew what was really going on, who was where, or even exactly how many people were still on the mountain from their own guided groups.

With all of the communication problems that happened in conjunction with this event, individual guides have to be commended for dealing with the situation they found themselves in and for getting all their clients back to camp safely. The guides compromised their own safety, exposing themselves to the elements in order to help their clients deal with the storm. They were able to navigate the route in zero visibility and did not let their clients stop moving downhill, even though some of them could not walk by the time they arrived at Camp Muir. The guides giving medical care at Camp Muir also did a great job in preventing further injury to their co-workers and for attending to the hypothermic woman and the other exhausted clients.

Although mountain forecasts can many times be wrong, they should never be taken lightly. A partly cloudy forecast can often become beautiful and sunny, or the forecasted ten mph winds can easily reach 40 mph, but when meteorologists are forecasting large upper level storm events, one can be generally certain some sort of unpleasant weather will happen. This was one of those events. The fact no one was killed and no one sustained permanent injury is a testament to the will and determination of all the people involved. (Source: Edited from a report by Cooper Self, Climbing Ranger)

AVALANCHE, POOR POSITION, IGNORED OBVIOUS POTENTIAL FOR AVALANCHE
Washington, Mount Rainier, Ingraham Direct

On the morning of June 5th at 0445, a large avalanche along the Ingraham Direct route was reported to NPS rangers by RMI guides on the Ingraham Glacier around 11,400 feet. Eleven people—a party of three Americans, a party of six Koreans, and two solo climbers, one of whom was a skier—were reported to have been involved in the avalanche. It was reported that five were still partially buried, five had been recovered, and one was still missing.

Rangers Glenn Kessler and Thomas Payne received the report at Camp Muir, whereupon Payne climbed to the scene while Kessler took the role of IC. When Ranger Payne arrived on scene, mountain guides and other members of the parties had recovered ten of the eleven involved climbers. Ranger Payne, along with guides from AAI, RMI, and IMG, assessed the injured climbers while plans were made for evacuation off the mountain.

Amazingly only three significant injuries resulted among the ten recovered climbers: a male (47) had been completely buried and lost consciousness, another male (62) complained of a knee injury, and another male (age unknown) had a facial laceration. The patient with the facial laceration was escorted to Camp Muir by a guide and later walked down to Paradise with the non-injured members of his party. Ranger Payne requested a helicopter evacuation for the remaining two patients. At 1218, a Chinook helicopter from Fort Lewis arrived on scene and evacuated the two injured climbers and remaining rescuers. The patients were taken directly to Madigan Hospital at Fort Lewis where they were treated for their injuries.

Due to remaining avalanche danger and the complex terrain above the slide, a ground search for the missing climber was deemed unsafe. A civilian MD530 helicopter was then used to conduct an aerial search of the slide path. Ranger Kessler boarded the civilian helicopter at Camp Muir and with the pilot and another observer conducted an aerial search. Gusty winds hampered the aircraft from getting close to the surface, but a mid-level search was completed, and provided no significant clues.

Over the next three days, rangers attempted to search for the missing climber. He had been the uppermost person on the route when the avalanche occurred. Stability and slope tests, however, indicated that the avalanche danger remained considerable to high at the elevation below the run-out of the avalanche and presumably at least that much above, thereby preventing rangers from safely accessing the debris area.

When the avalanche danger diminished to the point the area could be accessed with some degree of safety, rangers performed visual searches along with focused probing in likely catchment areas and debris build-up areas. No results were forthcoming.

Warm weather over the next couple of months caused melt-out of much of the debris, resulting in the surfacing of items lost in the avalanche. It is believed that all of these belonged to those who had survived the avalanche. Probe searching was completed around the areas where the melted-out items were located, but again, with no results.

Analysis

May and early June are often times of lingering unstable weather on Mount Rainier. However, it was exceptionally stormy during the early season. Storm after storm laid down layers of snow above 8,000 feet. With snowfall well above average and little time between storms for snow to settle, summit climbing of Mount Rainier was practically at a standstill due to avalanche danger. June 6th was one of the first days during this period to have a forecast for clear skies.

Having just climbed from Camp Muir to Ingraham Flats, the guided clients of RMI were learning about the potential avalanche danger. Their guides were explaining that they would be turning back due to this. Leaving the safety of Ingraham Flats was not a risk they would accept. It is likely that some of these clients saw the score of headlamps above them on the Ingraham Glacier Headwall and considered whether they had spent their money wisely on such tentative guides. Moments later, the slab avalanche ripped out and the debris came down to within a few hundred yards of Ingraham Flats.

The trigger of this avalanche is unknown, but it was likely a natural avalanche, as there was a great distance and elevation between the uppermost climber on-route and the crown. To choose to climb at a time when naturally triggered avalanches are possible is an even bigger error than to choose to climb when human-triggered avalanches are possible.

The one fatality that occurred was of a solo climber who was the highest on the route at the time. All the other injuries and burials that took place were of climbers lower in the run out zone, and this is possibly why many of them survived and were able to be found quickly by the guides nearby. The available rescue resources were tapped out dealing with searching, digging out those that survived and tending to the injured. By the time resources were freed up some 90 minutes later, the likelihood of finding the avalanche victim alive was less than ten percent.

There are many hazards on Mount Rainier, but there are only a few that climbers must take seriously enough to turn them around immediately. One of these is avalanche danger. On average, there are a dozen or so days during the typical climbing season where avalanche danger is so significant that it demands immediate action.

It is apparent that this avalanche would have resulted in more fatalities had there not been guides with avalanche safety training in the vicinity who acted rapidly. The fact that there were several parties on the upper mountain ignoring the obvious clues of avalanche danger speaks both to the goal orientation and level of commitment to achieve that goal that can blind-side climbers. Additionally, many independent climbers here lack avalanche knowledge and the mountaineering skills to manage the conditions. (Source: Edited from a report by Glenn Kessler, Climbing Ranger)

(Editor's Note: According to The Seattle Times on June 9, 2010, Mark Wedeven, 27, from Olympia was the missing climber. He had climbed Mount Rainier numerous times. He was solo climbing at the time.)

HAPE AND HACE
Washington, Mount Rainier, Camp Muir
On June 23 at 1745, rangers at Camp Muir were alerted of a climber (male, 49) who was having difficulty breathing after returning from a summit at-

tempt and resting in the public shelter.Rangers and a physician's assistant assessed the patient, consulted medical control, and concluded the man was suffering from high altitude pulmonary edema (HAPE). A decision was made to airlift the patient from Camp Muir, using a contract helicopter that was already in the park doing project work.

While rangers were preparing to fly the HAPE patient off the mountain, another report came in from guides at Ingraham Flats who were attending to an independent climber (female, 41) showing severe signs of high altitude cerebral edema (HACE), including rapidly decreasing levels of responsiveness. Due to the seriousness of the second patient's condition, a decision was made to fly her off the mountain also.

Analysis

High altitude pulmonary and cerebral edema can happen to anyone who is at altitude, and the only cure is to go to a lower elevation. Both patients were able to descend and get to definitive medical care in a timely manner. Patient care was expedited by experienced climbers and medical personnel who saw the signs of HAPE and HACE and reacted quickly.

One thing to note, though, is that the signs and symptoms of HAPE and HACE were not reported or reacted to early on by the people in the patients' climbing party but rather by other climbers and guides who happened to be on the mountain. In a popular mountain environment such as Mount Rainier, people often seem to rely on the presence and expertise of other more experienced climbers rather than using their own knowledge and skills to make decisions.

Another large contributing factor to altitude emergencies on Mount Rainier has to do with people living at relatively low elevations, then coming to the mountain and ascending from approximately sea level to 14,410 feet within 48 hours. These rapid ascents, especially when the person climbing might not have much experience with altitude, leaves little time for the body to properly acclimate. (Source: Edited from a report by Cooper Self, Climbing Ranger)

CLIMBER UNTIES FROM TEAM – DISAPPEARS DURING SEVERE WEATHER, INEXPERIENCED CLIMBING PARTNERS
Washington, Mount Rainier, Gibraltar Ledges

On the morning of July 1, Eric Lewis (57) went missing when his climbing companions discovered that he had unclipped from the climbing rope and disappeared. The three-man team was ascending the Gibraltar Ledges route and encountered high wind and low visibility. The climber in the lead, Don Storm, Jr., stopped and was joined by the second climber on the rope, Trevor Lane. At 13,900 feet, as they waited for Lewis to join them, they discovered only a coil with a butterfly knot when they reeled the rope in. They had caught glimpses of Lewis on the rope just moments before and immediately searched the slope below them. After what they deemed a thorough local search, they proceeded to the summit ridge in case Lewis had somehow skirted around them while they searched below. When Lewis was not found on the summit ridge, they returned to Camp Muir and reported the incident to climbing rangers.

Climbing ranger Tom Payne and two mountain guides climbed rapidly from Camp Muir to the summit looking for Lewis late Thursday (July 1st) afternoon. Arriving in the summit vicinity at 2000, the searchers looked for Lewis or any signs of his presence, but without any results. The search team returned to Camp Muir around 2200. Meanwhile, additional resources were sent up to Camp Muir Thursday afternoon to provide additional searchers and support personnel.

On Friday (July 2) the search expanded, with more than 40 personnel involved. Ground searchers included National Park Service climbing rangers, climbing guides from Rainier Mountaineering, Alpine Ascents International, and International Mountain Guides, as well as a few volunteers from Mountain Rescue. Park rangers aboard a military CH-47 Chinook helicopter from Fort Lewis and a contract helicopter from Northwest Helicopters searched from the air.

By mid-morning one team of ground searchers, which had focused its efforts on the 13,000–14,000-foot level, located the climber's backpack (containing climbing harness, snow shovel, and full but frozen water bottles) at 13,600 feet and then a tiny snowcave about 200 vertical feet above it. Another search team climbed and scoured the entire Gibraltar Ledges route along with the upper Nisqually and Ingraham Glaciers. A third search team concentrated efforts on the West side of the East crater rim, looking in the steam caves when possible.

Yet another search team consisting of rangers from Camp Schurman climbed up and over the Emmons route to thoroughly search the summit rim steams caves and then join the alpine search effort in the vicinity of the Ingraham Glacier and the Disappointment Cleaver.

On the third day of the search, both air and ground operations resumed. Rangers staged at Camp Muir continued the ground search operations, skiing to the base of Gibraltar Chute to search the area for signs of the missing climber. Having exhausted the searchable terrain on the Ingraham Glacier side the previous day, the ground search was refocused on the Nisqually Glacier side to cover the possibility that Lewis had fallen while down-climbing the Gibraltar Ledges or Gibraltar Chute routes. Rangers thoroughly examined the terrain in the fall line of these routes. They also explored the base of the Nisqually Icefall and the Muir Rocks Ridge leading up to the Gibraltar Chute, climbing up to and into the bergschrund under the chute.

Having searched the area extensively in and adjacent to the climber's last known location and having found no additional clues on the third day of the search, the likelihood of finding Lewis alive had diminished greatly. Given the very cold and very windy conditions during and following Lewis' disappearance and the lack of any emergency gear carried by the climber, survival in such harsh conditions for three days was unlikely. Weather models for what would be day four of the search indicated a front approaching with precipitation and high winds forecast on the mountain. Both air and ground search efforts would be curtailed by the incoming weather.

(Editor's Note: There was more narrative about the continuing and extensive searches. Mr. Lewis was not and has not yet been found.)

Analysis

Weather conditions had a lot to do with this incident, but the most significant contributing factors will probably never be known. The climber who unclipped from his partners' rope did so in very severe weather and for no known reason. Guesses included that he didn't want to slow his group down, had to deal with some personal problem, or had a mental lapse due to fatigue, hypothermia, or some altitude related illness. All were mentioned as possible reasons for him leaving the rope. It is also unknown how long Mr. Lewis was able to survive before succumbing to the cold or a fall from which he could not have survived. The discovery of his pack and a small "snow cave" high on the Ingraham Glacier provide clues that Mr. Lewis did survive for some time after losing contact with his party.

Lewis had left for his climb with very little in his pack, presumably to go "fast and light". As a result, Lewis had little to rely on when he separated from his team, especially given the weather conditions. He did not have a sleeping bag, tent, or any additional clothing beyond that which he had on his back.

While his party members did do a preliminary search when they realized Mr. Lewis was no longer on the rope, weather and inexperience hampered this effort. Mr. Lewis was actually the most experienced of the three climbers, although not the most fit of all of them. The area searched by the two climbers was just the radius of one rope from where they realized Mr. Lewis had gone missing. They did not feel comfortable backtracking even a few hundred feet down route, which was very likely the spot where Mr. Lewis had unclipped. By returning to Camp Muir and alerting NPS rangers to the situation, the climbers were able to summon people with more knowledge and experience to help search, but with the weather conditions and limited information on the exact location Mr. Lewis was last seen, search efforts were not successful.

Being able to navigate and deal with unexpected situations in all types of weather are required skills for traveling safely in mountain environments. Also, knowing yourself and your climbing partners' limitations are vital for successful climbing trips. (Source: Edited from a report by Glenn Kessler, Climbing Ranger)

HAPE – EXACERBATED BY PRE-EXISTING CHEST COLD
Washington, Mount Rainier, Emmons Route

On July 11 at 0930, Mount Rainier National Park received a distress call from three climbers high (13,500-foot level) on the Emmons Route. One of the climbers (30) was having difficulty walking and was showing signs and symptoms of high altitude pulmonary edema. Climbing Ranger Brian Hasebe was dispatched from the summit to respond and arrived on scene at 1015. The climber had passed out four times prior to caregiver arrival and six times post arrival. He was belayed and short-roped down the mountain with the assistance of two other park visitors. Climbing Ranger Jeremy Shank responded from Camp Schurman with additional medical supplies, including oxygen, which was administered at a flow rate of 12 LPM at 1330. While the patient's condition improved dramatically with the lower altitude and oxygen, his condition deteriorated rapidly with cessation of administered oxygen. The latter consideration strongly reinforced the decision to fly the patient from Camp Schurman immediately instead of arranging a time- and personnel-intensive ground evacuation. David Gottlieb coordinated helicopter operations, and the climber was airlifted by Northwest Helicopters from Camp Schurman at 1500 and transferred to an ALS unit.

Analysis

A preexisting medical condition (chest cold) strongly predisposed the climber to high altitude pulmonary edema. Once he succumbed to the condition, he was unable to self-evacuate, and without the assistance of nearby climbers, his condition would have necessitated a time-intensive rescue from the summit. Fortunately, a climbing ranger was already at the summit, descending an adjacent route, and was able to respond and coordinate the evacuation effort. (Source: Brian Hasebe, Climbing Ranger)

FALL ON SNOW – UNABLE TO SELF-ARREST, FALL INTO CREVASSE
Washington, Mount Rainier, Emmons Glacier

On July 27, a climbing party of four, including a father, his two teen-aged sons, and Lee Adams (52), was descending the Emmons glacier when one of the climbers tripped and fell. This caused the other climbers to be swept off their feet and, despite attempts to self-arrest, they slid approximately 100 feet on a steep slope and plummeted into a 35-foot-deep crevasse at about the 13,000-foot level. Two sustained minor injuries and one briefly lost consciousness and injured his right knee. Adams, the last man on the rope, died from traumatic injuries. The three surviving climbers were able to climb out of the crevasse and make their way back to Camp Schurman, the high camp at 9,450 feet, arriving at 1500. Climbing ranger David Gottlieb assessed the three climbers and contacted medical control. The party stayed at Camp Schurman for the night.

An MD 530 helicopter was ordered form Northwest Helicopters to assist in rescue and recovery operations the following day. The objectives of the operation were to evacuate the patient with a knee injury and insert rangers near the accident site and recover the body from the crevasse. It was planned for the remaining two climbers to be escorted off the mountain on foot.

Aviation operations began at 1130 on Wednesday. Climbing rangers David Gottlieb and Brian Scheele were dropped off by helicopter on the Winthrop saddle (13,600 feet) and made their way to the accident site. The retrieved body was airlifted off the mountain. The climber with the knee injury was also flown off the mountain. Ranger Ashby and the two uninjured climbers reached the White River Ranger Station at 1830. (Source: Nick Hall, edited by Climbing Ranger Cooper Self and ANAM editor)

Analysis

When climbers are roped together for protection, all members of the team have to be comfortable with the terrain on which they are traveling and with their ability to arrest the fall of any of their team members. Many times climbers are able to navigate these types of features without any negative consequence, but sometimes climbers may be unaware of the consequences a small fall could have on the entire group.

In situations where any member of the group feels he or she would not be able to arrest the fall of teammates, alternatives should be considered, including quick belays over crevasses or through steep areas and finding alternative routes with less exposure.

Mr. Adams was a very competent and experienced climber who tried with all his strength to stop the fall of his team, but his experience and strength alone were not enough to stop his teammates and himself from taking this ultimately fatal fall. (Source: Edited from a report by Nick Hall, Climbing Ranger)

(Editor's Note: In a post from KOMO TV and News Services, the following quote is noted: "Big shock… I'm just surprised it was Lee," said Fred Slater, a member of the Washington Alpine Club, where Adams helped teach for many years. "We all expected him to continue climbing well into his 60s. He was so fast. No one could ever keep up with Lee. He would out-climb and out-hike anybody.")

FALL ON SNOW
Washington, Mount Rainier, Disappointment Cleaver

On July 30 at 1130, Rangers received a 911 call from an independent climbing party at approximately 12,000 feet on the Disappointment Cleaver. The report was that one member of their party, Gary Fredrickson (age unknown) had slipped while descending the route and tumbled over rock and snow, injuring himself in the process. A response team of two guides left Camp Muir at 1200 with medical supplies to get an initial assessment of the patient. NPS climbing ranger Tom Payne, along with two guides, responded from Muir shortly after 1200 with more supplies and the plan of possibly flying the patient off of the mountain. Guides arrived on scene at 1311 and found the patient to have sustained injuries to his head and neck. Ranger Payne arrived on scene and packaged the patient on a backboard and into a litter capable of being hoisted into a helicopter. At 1555 an army reserve Chinook left Kautz heli-base with climbing rangers Scheele and Ashby on board. At 1612 the patient was hoisted into the aircraft and flown to Madigan Hospital where he was transferred to the emergency department.

Analysis

It is unknown whether fatigue, lack of experience, or environmental conditions contributed to this incident. The climbing route where the injury happened was in good shape, although warm snow conditions could have played a role. The climber was wearing a helmet when he fell, which very possibly saved him from further injury, as the helmet was cracked during the fall. He did sustain a fractured C-7 vertebra, but it was repaired with no known loss of neuro-functions. (Source: Edited from a report by Cooper Self, Climbing Ranger)

(Editor's Note: Ranger Cooper Self added the following: "In addition to the preceding reports, Climbing Rangers at Rainier responded to a number of other incidents during the 2010 season. Out of almost 10,000 climbers, there were 19 major SAR events involving climbers or day users above 8,000 feet on Rainier. These included eleven other rescues or assists. Four of these incidents involved broken bones and other less severe trauma. Rangers responded to seven medical calls where patients needed assistance from the NPS, including cardiac arrest, diabetic emergencies, and various respiratory and altitude related emergencies. There were also four searches conducted for overdue climbing parties that eventually showed up under their own power or were found with no injury. Climbing rangers also responded to numerous medical calls and rescues and visitor assists in the lower elevations of Mount Rainier National Park.")

ROCK FOOTHOLD CAME LOOSE – FALL ON ROCK
Washington, North Cascades, Vesper Peak

(The following account is edited from a narrative submitted by Steph Abegg, 27.)

At 5:00 a.m. on September 14, I pulled up at my sister Jenny's house in Seattle. We were on our way to what we planned to be a fun and relatively mellow end-of-summer climb of the North Face of Vesper. We were at the trailhead by 7:00 a.m. and at the saddle looking at the north face of Vesper at 9:20 a.m. The moats did not look like they would be a problem on the glacier below, so we decided to cross the glacier and do the entire route. Once off the glacier, we began to climb the north face route. It was a bit wet in areas so we had to bypass on the right of the actual route. This was taking quite a bit of time, but we saw a reasonable way up to where the bypass ledge hit the upper route.

The accident occurred at 1:00 p.m. I was about 20 feet above the belay on 5.7–5.8 terrain. I had set three pieces of protection and was roped on a doubled 8-mm. Suddenly, a rock flake I was standing on broke loose. I felt my left ankle rotate inwards, either as my foot was caught between some rocks or the ankle was torqued out by the rockfall. As I fell, I remember thinking, "My foot is hurt bad. This is not good." I fell cleanly about 15 feet before the rope caught on my highest piece, which had not pulled. I looked down and could see my left foot flopping and my splintered tibia sticking through the inner ankle. Blood and yellowish-white fluid was flowing, but not spurting.

I immediately asked Jenny to lower me down to a stand of bushes we had passed about 20 feet below where I could be somewhat safe and comfortable. I clipped myself to a bush. After trying to retrieve as much gear as possible, Jenny lowered down, clipped herself to the bushes, pulled the rope, and wrapped it around a small tree she would eventually rappel off. I was already starting to shake with the initial stages of shock, so Jenny helped me put on a couple of insulated jackets, a hat, and some wool gloves.

We quickly turned our attention to the foot. We were not sure to what extent it was bleeding, so we created a couple makeshift tourniquets around my thigh and upper calf with slings. (I later found out one of my arteries had been severed by the broken bones) We decided to use an ice ax as a splint. I rotated the foot into place and Jenny wrapped a fleece jacket tightly around the foot and ice ax splint. This was quite painful and I could hear the shattered bones grinding together as I told her to pull as tight as she could. We also used crampon straps to cinch the fleece even tighter against the leg. Initially I propped the foot against my other knee with the tip of the ice ax that was sticking out, but I later tied my foot to the tree above me in an attempt to minimize the bleeding, which was a worrisome constant drip. I draped my legs with my rain shell to keep them as warm as possible. We transferred all of the food and water into my backpack and I gave her my car key.

After Jenny left, I felt quite alone and exposed on the mountain. (Jenny later told me that after she left me was one of the loneliest times of her life as well; but it was her willingness to go get help alone that saved my life.) To keep myself occupied, I made words with some alphabet cookies I had brought. I fiddled with my camera, took some photos of my foot tied to the bush, and rustled around in the backpack deciding what I didn't want to leave behind on the mountain. I also ate most of the energy bars Jenny had left me with, mainly because it was just another thing to do other than focusing on the pain. There was a very real possibility that Jenny would not be able to alert a rescue team for several hours, so I knew it was important to keep my wits about me. I wondered how I would keep myself occupied when my alphabet cookies were gone.

Fortunately, Jenny could yell to me the entire time she was making her way to the glacier and the saddle. She reached the saddle around 3:00 p.m. Her heart dropped when she could not get a cell signal. So she continued up the ridge towards the summit, checking her phone constantly. Not far up the ridge, her efforts were rewarded when her phone showed a couple of bars of service. Jenny immediately called 9-1-1. When she mentioned this was a mountain rescue, she was transferred to the Snohomish County Sheriff's Office Air Operations Helicopter Rescue Team. She requested a short haul.

The helicopter arrived at 3:40 p.m. After identifying my position (they were a bit thrown off that I was the actual injured climber when I started to take photos of them), they dropped one of their party to the bushes below. Ernie attached me to a seat harness and by 4 p.m. I was lifted into the helicopter. They then flew directly to Providence Regional Medical Center in Everett, arriving there around 5:00 p.m. I was on the operating table for several hours undergoing open reduction to put pins and plates in my leg, to do artery reconstruction, and to perform an emergency fasciotomy. I am forever thankful and indebted to the whole-hearted efforts of the surgeons and the SCSO AirOps Helicopter Rescue Team.

Analysis

The cell phone call was vital to the success of the rescue, as the doctors told me I probably would have lost my foot had I been up there much longer. Moreover, with the poor weather throughout most of the following week, it was unclear whether an airlift could have been conducted the next day.

The outcome could have been very different had it not been for several factors, including but not limited to:
- I was not climbing alone.
- We were roped up and I had set good protection.
- Jenny and I both kept calm when the accident occurred.
- We made a game plan for rescue.
- We were competent with first aid and anchors.
- Jenny was willing and able to descend alone to get help.
- I was resigned to stay on the mountain alone and take care of myself while Jenny went for rescue.
- We had a cell phone.
- Jenny was able to get to a place with cell service (Verizon).
- We had good weather.

- We had started climbing early enough in the day so that the accident occurred with enough time to get an airlift before darkness.

After an accident, there are always the "what ifs" and "should haves." I do not feel we made any poor decisions the day of the accident, but if I could do it all over again there are a couple of things I would do differently:

- I would have climbed only the upper section of the route. The lower half—where the accident occurred—turned out to be loose, poorly protected, and not very aesthetic. We had decided to climb the lower section since we wanted to climb the whole route rather than cutting in midway.
- I would have had a SPOT or PLD with me. Although the cell phone allowed us to verbally communicate with the rescue team to let them know the details of the accident and location, we were lucky that Jenny found a cell signal.

FALL ON ICE, INADEQUATE PROTECTION – TOOL PLACEMENT
Washington, Banks Lake, Brush Bash

On 30 December, RM (23), while leading Brush Bash, WI 4, (one pitch) at Banks Lake, Washington, sustained a leader fall resulting in a badly sprained left ankle. The overnight temperature was close to 0 F, and the daytime temperature reached about 25 F. The day was clear and sunny, and the ice was well formed.

Earlier in the day three others and I drove to Banks Lake and were in the same area. I led Brush Bash that morning, and with two ropes set up a top rope for my companions to practice their skills. Later than morning RM and BC (23) arrived and hiked up to meet us. BC, an experienced and technically solid ice climber, first led a nearby WI 5+ route, which I followed. RM was still relatively new to technical ice climbing. RM and BC then moved over to Brush Bash so RM could get more time on ice and practice leading.

Brush Bash has a solidly vertical section about half way up. RM placed a screw at the base of that section. About two thirds of the way up that section, RM experienced difficulty. He placed a high tool and then placed his other tool very close to the first. The ice around both tools then "dinner plated". As a result, RM sustained a fall of approximately 20–25 feet. His screw at the base of the vertical section held his fall, but he caught his left ankle and bounced coming to a rest head down, shaken, and in pain. At first he thought, as did the rest of us, that his ankle was broken.

BC lowered RM to the ground, where I splinted his lower leg and ankle using one of his tools and perlon (the rough "L" shape of an ice tool approximates the lower leg/ankle/foot alignment). One of the people with me was a retired nurse who treated RM for shock. My three companions further stabilized RM and began slowly assisting him down the talus slope to the car (about 150 meter/450 foot descent). BC belayed me while I climbed

Brush Bash to clean R's screws and draws, and retrieve the rope. All of RM's screws (five up to the point of the fall) were acceptable placements, though several could have been better placed, and the draw on the screw below the one that held RM was twisted and "back clipped" to the rope.

BC transported RM to the hospital where the diagnosis was a badly sprained ankle.

Analysis

Two factors contributed to RM's fall. One factor was technical, the other psychological. The technical factor was placing his tools too close together. The psychological factor was RM was clearly not comfortable leading. Up to the point of his fall, he verbalized to BC his lack of confidence and uncertainty.

RM demonstrated stoicism and maturity throughout. Though obviously in great pain, he did not lose consciousness and contributed to his own self-extraction. All of the rescuers used clear thinking, good first aid skills, and cooperative teamwork. The result is that within a fairly short time an injured climber was safely evacuated to medical care by a team of self-reliant climbers. (Source: Bob Loomis, 56, Spokane, Washington)

FALL ON ROCK, EQUIPMENT FAILURE DUE TO MIS-USE
West Virginia, New River Gorge, Kaymoor

On June 12 Karen Feher (33) and her partner were climbing Rico Suave (5.10a). Upon reaching the anchor, she clipped in. Her setup: She had two thin dyneema slings girth hitched to her harness. At the end of each sling was a locking carabiner held in place with a rubber Petzl keeper (called 'Petzl Strings'). The "string" is designed to fit on the end of a Petzl runner in order to keep the lower carabiner on a quickdraw in place for easy clipping and to protect the webbing from abrasion.

She clipped a locking carabiner to each bolt and probably called, "Off belay." It is unclear if she was going to rappel or be lowered. It doesn't matter. She took a fatal fall about 50 feet to the ground.

The day after the accident, a local climber climbed to the anchor and found a locking carabiner on each bolt with a Petzl String still affixed to each. Both Petzl Strings were torn on the side. It is unclear if the two slings were still attached to her harness, as her harness went with her and EMS, but I am assuming this to be true.

Analysis

How could this happen? This is one of the safest setups for cleaning an anchor. At the top of Rico Suave is a small ledge to stand on and clean. If you're not fully weighting the system, these rubber strings will hold about 15 pounds before breaking. I'm guessing they were able to hold just enough weight to feign security while she untied to feed, until just enough weight was added to cause the break.

There is some level of speculation, but with the evidence at hand this seems to be the most likely scenario. (Source: Mike Williams, from a post on rockclimbing.com, and http://www.dailymail.com/News)

AVALANCHE
Wyoming, Grand Teton National Park, South Teton

On February 22 at 1120, Wray Landon (31) was caught in an avalanche and carried to his death while skiing near the summit of the South Teton. Landon was skiing with partners Nathan Brown (32) and Brady Johnston (27). Both searched the slide path for Landon immediately after the avalanche occurred. They descended the path to the edge of a steep cliff where they could see something in the debris field over 1000 feet below, though they could not tell if it was Landon. At that point, Brown called 911 and was connected to Park Dispatch. Park rangers and several Teton County Search and Rescue (TCSAR) personnel responded to the scene using the Teton County Sheriff's Office rescue helicopter.

At 1335, rangers located the debris field and Landon's body, and while hovering nearby, determined that Landon was deceased. TCSAR personnel used explosives which were dropped from the helicopter to control slopes that rangers would have to cross over or under to reach the body. Rangers were flown to a staging area at Snowdrift Lake where they then skied to the body. The body was extricated via helicopter long line to the valley and the rescue rangers were picked up at Snowdrift Lake and flown back to the Jackson Hole Airport.

I talked to Brown by cell phone and told him to descend Garnet Canyon via the route they had climbed that morning. Johnston and Brown skied back to the Taggart Lake Trailhead without further incident, arriving at 1600.

Analysis

Under mostly sunny skies at the summit, these ski mountaineers discussed their options. They considered skiing the Southeast Couloir, but were concerned that with its east and south exposure, it would be sun crusted and not very enjoyable skiing. The second option was to ski the South Face, which also had the potential for sun crusts given its aspect. Everyone in the party knew that one of the south couloirs, known as the Amore Vita, had been skied two days before by a party of two. The group could still see the ski tracks in the snow and Brown had spoken to a member of that party, Steve Romeo, about the conditions. The group felt that the Amore Vita was their best option because it had been previously skied and would likely provide better and safer snow conditions because it was protected from direct sunlight. Johnston told me that he and Landon had skied that line together about three times in the past. Brown told me that he had skied the South Face one time before.

After the group settled on the Amore Vita, they started down towards the South Face one at a time. Johnston went first, and Brown noted that he was aggressively jumping on the snow above the Southeast Couloir testing its stability. They found that only a shallow sun crust would break up and slide away. The group continued to descend to the skier's right of the Southeast Couloir on a steep slope described by Brown to be around 50 degrees. The group was spread out as they reached the top portion of the South Face. Johnston was in the lead, followed by Landon and then Brown. They traversed one at a time, high across the top of the South Face snowfield, ski cutting and jumping on the slope to test stability. They regrouped on a 20 to 25 degree portion of the slope high on the skier's right side. The main portion of the South Face snowfield was below them, later estimated to be about 35 degrees. From his previous descent of the South Face, Brown recognized that the slope held "way more snow" than he had seen there before, and he said that to the group. On the slope, they could clearly see the two sets of tracks left the by the group that had skied the Amore Vita.

Johnston skied the slope first, moving left towards the middle of the slope before turning back to the right towards the entrance to the Amore Vita. He told me that he was skiing "light" because the snow definitely felt weird. He noted that they were aware that there was a wind slab on the slope. In relation to the previous tracks on the slope, Johnston said that he was basically skiing the same line. He arrived at the entrance to the Amore Vita and looked back up to Landon and Brown. Landon yelled down to Johnston that he thought he could enter the Amore Vita from where he was standing with Brown, but Johnston yelled back that that was not the best way in. (Note: It is apparently possible to enter the Amore Vita at that point, however the route is more difficult and would require technical down climbing and significant exposure.) Brown said that Landon then looked at him, turned away and started skiing. He said he thinks Landon made about two or three turns when he heard a "whumpf." Brown realized that a slab avalanche had broken right under his own skis, and he quickly worked to step uphill off of the blocks that were moving under his feet. Brown managed to stop on the bed surface near the avalanche crown. He did not hear any sound from Landon, and when he was able to look up, he could not see Landon.

In my separate interview with Johnston, he guessed that Landon was four to eight turns into the run when the avalanche occurred. He said that Landon appeared to be skiing the same line that he had, or possibly a little to the skier's left of his line. When the avalanche occurred, Johnston noted that "the slide released really quickly," and he could not see Landon in it at all. He described the slide as being so quick that it seemed to suck the air along with it. A powder cloud developed, and Johnston, who was standing on rocks, was showered with snow.

Brown recalled that immediately after the avalanche, he was yelling down to Johnston, though he couldn't remember what he was saying. Brown then opened his transceiver and realized that it did not appear to be working. He looked to Johnston who also had his transceiver out and was moving into a search pattern on the slide path. Brown followed behind Johnston and scanned the slide path for signs of Landon. Fewer than ten minutes had elapsed since the avalanche occurred, and at that point Brown made the 911 call.

While some people consider the type of ski mountaineering that Landon was doing to be inherently dangerous, those of us who enjoy this activity understand the associated risks and work hard to mitigate them. The hazards can be many and include rock fall, fatigue, falls, equipment failure, weather and avalanches.

Landon's party was well prepared both in experience and with equipment. All three members of the party had skied on the South Teton before, as well as having done many other ski mountaineering descents in the Teton Range. They were informed as to the current and past snow conditions. They had talked to the party that skied the Amore Vita two days before and they had discussed their intended route and associated hazards before they began skiing. All three members of the party were extremely fit and mentally prepared for their skiing objective. There is no evidence that peer pressure, haste, or any overwhelming drive to complete the objective clouded their judgment. They realized that the slope they were skiing was a wind loaded slab. They ski cut and kicked at the slope as they crossed it one at a time. Unfortunately, when Landon began skiing, he most likely initiated the slide that killed him by impacting what many avalanche professionals call a "sweet spot," or an area of weakness in the snow pack that when affected can initiate a fracture. This was an unfortunate accident in which Landon made a calculated risk and paid the ultimate price. (Source: Scott Guenther, Incident Commander)

ICE COLUMN COLLAPSE – FALL ON ICE, LATE SEASON
Wyoming, Yellowstone National Park, Grand Canyon of the Yellowstone

On May 25, Mark Ehrich (28) and Michael Kellch (29) died when a frozen waterfall called Silver Cord Cascade collapsed while they were climbing it.

Steve Langlas, of the construction company Langlas and Associates, which employed both men, said Kellch and Ehrich were childhood friends in Casper and were living together in Bozeman. They were experienced ice climbers.

Analysis

Silver Cord Cascade is about three miles downstream of the Upper Falls of the Yellowstone. Joe Josephson of Livingston, who has climbed Silver Cord and has written a book about ice climbing in southern Montana and northern Wyoming, said climbers ski to the site from Artist's Point, rappel down and then climb back up. Generally speaking, it's not considered all that difficult a climb, he said, but "it's quite spectacular." He also stated, "… but ice conditions can change so quickly that it's hard to say what the difficulty is from day to day."

Silver Cord would be frozen nearly solid in midwinter, Josephson said, but from March on, the flow of water beneath the ice grows steadily and can make climbing conditions dangerous.

Hiking and climbing in the Grand Canyon of the Yellowstone are prohibited from the brink of the Upper Falls downriver to the Silver Cord Cascade drainage. Park rangers said climbers attempt Silver Cord Cascade maybe one to three times a year. (Source: Yellowstone National Park News Release)

DISLODGED ROCK – FALL ON ROCK, FATIGUE
Wyoming, Grand Teton, Black Dike

On July 17 around 1200, Paul Iman (23) contacted Rangers G.R. Fletcher and D. Hardesty at the Lower Saddle of Garnet Canyon. He was returning from the Black Dike area about a quarter of a mile above the Lower Saddle where he had earlier dislodged a rock while scrambling upward and fallen a short distance. After he had fallen, a rock impacted his rib area causing bruising. While descending to the Lower Saddle, he had further experienced severe fatigue and nearly fainted.

D. Hardesty immediately contacted Rescue Coordinator G. Montopoli about the situation and Iman was escorted to the Lower Saddle Ranger hut. Rangers administered oxygen, food, and water over the course of the next couple hours. Park Medical Director Dr. Will Smith was also contacted via cell phone by the rangers at the Lower Saddle and apprised of the situation. Dr. Smith advised that Iman be escorted to the valley by rangers so they could monitor his injuries.

At 1400, after receiving substantial amounts of food and water from the rangers, Iman decided that his medical status had significantly improved and refused any further medical assistance from the rangers. He instead returned to his camp at the Moraine camping zone below the Lower Saddle, aware that the rangers would be spending the night at the Lower Saddle should his health deteriorate. The rescue was terminated at 1400. (Source: George Montopoli, Incident Commander)

Analysis

The approach to the actual rock climbing on the Grand Teton has to be treated with great care, both on the ascent in the dark and on the descent after having been out for many hours. Loose rocks abound here. (Source: Jed Williamson)

FALL ON SNOW, UNABLE TO SELF-ARREST, INEXPERIENCE
Wyoming, Grand Teton National Park, Paintbrush Divide

On July 18, at about 1350, Stewart Laing (47) slid about 30 feet on snow, then cart-wheeled another 75–100 feet on talus near the summit of Paintbrush Divide (east side) after the snow that he was crossing collapsed. He suffered a significant injury involving an open, tibia-fibula fracture to his left leg. He was on overnight excursion and carrying a large pack. He had left with his brother, Jim Laing (50), earlier that day from the Lower Paintbrush camping zone.

After stabilizing S. Laing with the help of two hikers, J. Laing ran down Paintbrush Canyon until he was able to call out via cell phone. He was placed in contact with Rescue Coordinator G. Montopoli via Grand Teton Dispatch. After a brief interview with J. Laing, Montopoli immediately initiated a rescue operation at 1515 via a Jenny Lake page and requested the contract helicopter.

Ranger J. Springer ran Operations at the Lupine Rescue Cache, while Rangers J. McConnell and R. Schuster were flown to the scene with R. Johnson acting as spotter. The helicopter landed on a snowfield on the west side of the top of the divide at 1620. McConnell and Schuster hiked to the accident scene about 200 feet below the Paintbrush Divide summit. After medically evaluating the injuries to S. Laing, contacting Medical Director Dr. Will Smith, surveying the scene, and discussing rescue options, a helicopter short-haul was determined to be the best method of evaluation.

S. Laing was extracted from the accident site and flown unattended to the snowfield at the top of Paintbrush Divide. He was then flown to the Lupine Meadows Rescue Cache, transferred to the Park Ambulance and transported to St. John's Medical Center in Jackson for advanced medical care. (Source: George Montopoli, Incident Commander)

Analysis

This traverse is a very popular route and is done both west to east and east to west. Usually the snow is gone by the end of July. But if it isn't, a different level of mountaineering skill is required.

At least this hiker, who became a climber because of the conditions, had an ice ax with him and he had it in hand. However, due to inexperience, he was unable to self-arrest when he fell on his back. (Source: Jed Williamson)

FALL ON ROCK, CLIMBING ALONE, OFF ROUTE, NO CLIMBING EXPERIENCE
Wyoming, Grand Teton National Park, Garnet Canyon

On July 20, Jillian Drow (21) fell to her death while descending into the South Fork of Garnet Canyon after an ascent of the Middle Teton.

Drow was a member of a party of eight that left the Lupine Meadows Trailhead at approximately 0500. Seven people planned on climbing the southwest couloir of the Middle Teton and one person in the group was attempting a climb of the Grand Teton. Of the seven climbers attempting the Middle Teton, only Drow and Paul Riak (21) summited. Drow and Riak began descending the SW couloir. Drow was moving faster than Riak and the two made a plan to meet in the Garnet Meadows, Drow going ahead. Riak continued descending to the Meadows, where he met the rest of his group, and Drow had not yet arrived. One member of their party went up the South Fork of Garnet Canyon to look for Drow, and Riak and Jen Cotton left to find cell service lower in the canyon, to call GRTE Dispatch. About 2100, a member of their group, M. Domeier, located Drow's body at the base of a cliff. Domeier relayed this information to Cotton, who informed the SAR Coordinator of Drow's probable death. Rangers hiked up Garnet Canyon, arriving at the scene at 0130 and determined that Drow was deceased. Drow's body was flown from Garnet Canyon to Lupine Meadows the following day.

Analysis

Jillian Drow was an accomplished athlete, but very unfamiliar with the hazards of the mountain environment. Why this tragic event happened and how a similar event could be prevented in the future merits discussion.

The route Drow chose that led her to the cliff where she fell was a very different route than the one she ascended that morning when climbing the Middle Teton. Being aware of your surroundings is essential to traveling safely in the mountains, and it is especially important when in terrain one has not seen before. If a route was reasonable on the ascent, it generally should be followed on the descent.

Traveling alone is never a good idea in the mountains, especially if one has limited experience. Had Drow and Riak stayed together on their descent, the outcome may have been different. Riak followed Drow's tracks to near the top of the cliff and he was able to go around the cliff, thinking it too steep to descend. If the two were together, it is likely they would have both gone around the cliff.

Drow had already had a long day in the mountains. She had begun hiking at 0500 from the Lupine Meadows trailhead and was on the summit of the peak at 1600 hours. She knew the other members of her original group were waiting for her in the Meadows and she may have felt pressured to make haste to keep that group from waiting. Any pressure she may have put on herself, combined with possible fatigue from a long day in the mountains, may have contributed to this tragic outcome.

The Southwest Couloir of the Middle Teton is a non-technical climbing route, but it is easy for a hiker to get on technical terrain if careful route-finding is not practiced. Many hikers attempting an ascent/descent of this couloir have found themselves in technical terrain without the experience or equipment to cope safely, and many SAR missions have been conducted to rescue these climbers.

A wealth of information in the form of photographs, written descriptions, and personal experience can be found at the Jenny Lake Ranger Station. Climbers beginning their apprenticeship in the Teton Range can benefit greatly from this resource. (Source: Marty Vidak, Incident Commander)

LIGHTNING – IGNORED CLOUD BUILD UP, POOR POSITION, FALL ON ROCK, UNKNOWN RAPPEL ERROR – EXACERBATED BY COLD HANDS AND INEXPERIENCE
Wyoming, Grand Teton National Park, Grand Teton

Prior to the beginning of this storm, members of all parties described an awareness of the approaching clouds. A series of lightning strikes shocked several people and the parties decided to sit tight in hopes that the storm would pass quickly. The storm intensity increased and both the Tyler party (five members who were "determined to sit it out") and the Sparks party (eight members) began to move down the mountain with the intention of finding protection from the wind, rain and lightning. The Tyler party was in the Owen Chimney area and the Sparks party was in the Double Chimney area lower on the Owen-Spalding route. The Kline party remained near the Boulder Problem in the Sky at the top of the Exum Ridge route, well above the other parties.

A series of very strong lightning bolts hit the mountain during this time (about 1215). In the Sparks party, Greg Sparks descended to below the double chimneys and prepared an anchor. Brandon Oldenkamp (21) was belayed to Greg Sparks (55) who clipped Brandon into a figure eight on a bight with a carabiner to Brandon's harness. A large bolt of lightning occurred and Greg Sparks was knocked down. He observed Brandon falling over the edge of the mountain. Only one other member of Spark's party was injured (electrical, minor).

In the Owen Chimney area the Tyler party was in the process of rappelling down the Owen Chimney. They were hoping to sit out the storm at the top of the chimney, but after some shocks from lightning and the increased winds and rain, they decided to descend. Dan Tyler had rappelled down the chimney and was near the base when two shocks occurred. He heard that two members of his party above were affected, so he started up to help when more large shocks occurred. He was knocked down and had no feeling in his legs and one arm as well as burns to his back. He immediately called 911 and was connected to the Park Dispatch at 1223.

Above him, Troy Smith (40) was unconscious and in respiratory arrest (NB: Steve Tyler was temporarily unable to move but soon was giving Troy Smith mouth-to-mouth resuscitation. Smith began breathing after about ten breaths from Steve Tyler, 67). Henry Appleton (31) was thrown to the ground and unable to move his right leg. Mike Tyler (41) was relatively un-injured and descended the mountain, traversing the lower Owen-Spalding area tied in with the Sparks party to summon help.

At the top of the Exum Ridge, the Kline party was gathered in an alcove. They were squatting away from their ice axes and climbing gear and felt several shocks, then one large one that sent them all sprawling. Alan Kline (27) was knocked unconscious temporarily. He had minor burns on his right leg and had major internal injuries. (He was later admitted to the ICU with air around his heart and esophagus.) Betsy Smith (26) lost all feeling from her body and had a serious burn injury to one hand and was unable to use the other, even after some recovery. (Her right index finger was amputated in the ICU.) Matthew Walker (21) was coherent but unable to walk. He sustained bad burns to a foot, arm, and his rib cage. Andrew Larson was uninjured and climbed down and rappelled the 100 foot rappel to the Upper Saddle where he joined Mike Tyler. They continued to the Lower Saddle, ahead of the Sparks Party, to summon help.

The Teton Interagency Dispatch Center received 911 calls forwarded from surrounding counties starting at 1223. SAR coordinator Chris Harder had the Jenny Lake Rescue team paged out at 1227.

While the rescue plan was being developed, the Kline party was working their way down the upper mountain by lowering and rappelling, including one roped, pendulum fall by Matt Walker.

At 1354 Helicopter 7HE dropped Rangers Helen Bowers and Jack Mc-Connell at the Lower Saddle and then conducted an aerial reconnaissance of the accident scene. Conditions were not safe for insertion of rangers at the scene so at 1416, Bowers and McConnell started up the mountain on foot with Exum guide Dan Corn. At 1430, rangers Vidak, Visnovske, and Guenther were dropped at the Lower Saddle. Guenther was assigned Op-erations Chief at the Lower Saddle, while Vidak and Visnovske headed up the mountain. McConnell and Bowers soon met with members of the Kline and Tyler parties below the Black Dike and gained additional information. Below the Upper Saddle McConnell saw two members of the Sparks party rappelling down the Idaho Express snow chute. McConnell instructed them to ascend and wait for other rescuers to direct them down the normal descent.

Rangers Hardesty, Armitage, and Schuster were dropped at the Lower Saddle at 1447 and began ascending the mountain. As rangers met with the Sparks party, they guided them through various parts of the descent to the Lower Saddle. At 1520 McConnell and Corn began the Belly Roll at the beginning of the technical section of the Owen-Spalding route. Traversing the long ledge system, they were subjected to jets of water gushing from cracks in the cliff side. They arrived at the base of the Owen Chimney at 1537 and began a quick examination of Dan Tyler (40). McConnell transmitted that conditions were favorable for short-haul extraction. Guide Dan Corn secured Dan Tyler while McConnell continued up to the other patients.

Ranger Rick Guerrieri with Exum Guides Brenton Reagan and Anneka Door were dropped off at the Lower Saddle by the Yellowstone Llama helicopter. An external sling load of rescue equipment was flown to the base of Sergeants Chimney near the accident scene by Helicopter 7HE. One Teton Interagency Helitack crew member John Filardo, Ranger Case Martin, and A.J. Wheeler, MD, followed to the Lower Saddle.

At 1545 Ranger Bowers arrived at the Upper Saddle and saw Elizabeth Smith being lowered down the 100-foot rappel and aided her at the bottom. The other two members of the Kline party followed. Rangers Vidak, Hardesty, Schuster, Visnovske, and Armitage arrived at the Upper Saddle during this time. Visnovske, as Medical Unit Leader, remained at the Saddle with Bowers to aid the injured members of the Kline party while the others continued up the Owen-Spalding route.

At 1648 the first pair of patients were extracted from the top of the Owen Chimney via Screamer Suit/Short-Haul. Rangers Vidak and Hardesty arrived at the base of the Owen Chimney and began care of Dan Tyler. Rangers Armitage and Schuster continued up to aid McConnell.

At 1706 all of the Sparks party had arrived at the Lower Saddle. At this point a large thunderstorm moved over the area and all aerial operations were suspended. Heavy rain and winds and lightning lashed and shocked the rescuers and their patients for an hour and a half. The weather cleared enough to resume operations and the patient at the base of the Owen Chimney, Dan Tyler, was short-hauled off the mountain to the Lower Saddle at 1845 hours. Rangers McConnell, Armitage, Schuster, and Guide Dan Corn moved the final patient from the Tyler party to the 100-foot rappel of the Owen-Spalding and lowered him to the Upper Saddle. These actions cleared all patients from the mountain above the Upper Saddle.

At 1858 two patients were short-hauled from the Upper Saddle to the Lower Saddle. At 1915 the final two patients were short-hauled from the Upper Saddle to the Lower Saddle. All rescuers except Visnovske, Armitage, and McConnell descended toward the Lower Saddle at this time. Shuttles of patients, then rescuers, continued from the Lower Saddle to Lupine Meadows with all patients down by 1956 hours.

Helicopter 7HE was then used to sweep the Exum Ridge and popular Teton routes for possible other parties in distress. The helicopter then moved into Valhalla Canyon and the Black Ice-West Face areas to search for Brandon Oldenkamp, but met with no success. Air operations were ended as the daylight faded. All rescue personnel except Visnovske, Armitage, and

McConnell, who had descended to the Lower Saddle and remained there for the night, were off the mountain.

On the morning of July 22 the aerial search continued with Helicopter 7HE. Oldenkamp's body was found quickly and a ground team was assembled to move him to a location where he could be air lifted. Rangers Jernigan, Schuster, Vidak, Guenther, and Hardesty were flown to Valhalla Canyon and ascended to the scene. The deceased was lowered three hundred feet over moderately steep scree then air lifted from there and delivered to the Teton County Coroner at the Rudd's Picnic Area in Lupine Meadows. The rangers were flown back to Lupine Meadows. Rescue equipment was then flown down from the Lower Saddle but attempts to retrieve equipment from the upper mountain were unsuccessful due to high winds.

An attempt was made to retrieve equipment via long line from the upper mountain on July 23, but high winds precluded the operation. Early July 24, Ranger Drew Hardesty climbed to the Upper Saddle to attach the rescue equipment sling load. He then descended to the Lower Saddle and was flown back to Lupine Meadows.

Analysis

Brandon Oldenkamp had some experience with technical rock climbing and had used his harness and belay equipment in a trip to the Black Hills in 2009. On July 19th Brandon was in a group that ascended the Middle and South Tetons. They returned to their camp in the Garnet Meadows that night. On July 20th the group moved their camp two thousand feet higher to the Moraines camp zone arriving between noon 1200 and 1300. Mr. Oldenkamp was very fit and was not noticed to be fatigued or overly tired. He spent the day around camp eating well and in good spirits. Brandon slept well under the stars and awakened in apparently good shape and good spirits on the 21st. The group left camp around 0500. and Brandon was moving well, scrambling easily up the rock to the Upper Saddle. The party moved across the initial technical pitch of the Owen Spalding route as some snow began to fall. Brandon had no trouble negotiating the climbing and arrived at the base of the Owen Chimney with no difficulty.

According to Barry Sparks (52), the first lightning bolt was felt by everyone, though it is not certain what Mr. Oldenkamp experienced. The group decided to descend the mountain and Greg Sparks was belayed down to the base of the double chimney. Greg established an anchor and tied a figure eight on a bight for Brandon, who was being belayed from above down to Greg's location.

Greg Sparks clipped the figure eight loop into Brandon's harness with a carabiner. A large bolt of lightning struck at this time (about a half an hour since the first shock). Greg Sparks was thrown to the ground and he saw Brandon Oldenkamp thrown out and down the cliff out of sight.

Conclusions: Lightning storms are common in the Teton Range in the summer. Although most storms occur in the afternoon or evening and follow a distinct progression, storms at other times of the day or night are not rare and are often missed by professional weather forecasters. All three parties in this incident made a decision to ignore obvious signs of an impending storm: dark clouds, rapidly increasing in size from a relatively clear morning sky. Seasoned Teton climbers have the knowledge and/or experience to rapidly move to less exposed terrain when the first signs of building clouds appear.

The Tyler and Kline parties both decided to wait out what they felt was going to be a rapidly passing disturbance. As the storm increased in intensity, they sought shelter from the snow, rain and wind by huddling near alcoves of rock. Their actions put them into areas much more likely to be subject to electrical currents from lightning, specifically near rock walls and overhangs. The Sparks party made an earlier decision to descend but was still caught by the storm. They also sought protection from the elements. They moved down into the Double Chimney area of the Owen Spalding route, making them much more likely to experience electrical shocks from lightning.

Why Brandon Oldenkamp's tie-in failed is difficult to confirm, but evidence points to an improper attachment to his harness. Hypothermia, cold hands, lack of experience and the intensity of the situation were all contributing factors. However, based on the physical evidence, it appears that Oldencamp's gear loops were pulled on hard enough and quickly enough to break its attachment to the harness and strip off a piece of the tubing that it was laced through. A second possibility is that Brandon was tied into the figure of eight climbing rope loop on the gate side of the locking carabiner. The violence of his reaction to the electrical shock could have caused the rope to come out of the carabiner if it was not in the locked position.

It should be noted that this rescue began about one hour after the conclusion of the recovery of Jillian Drow, a rescue that began the night before. (Source, Jim Springer, Incident Commander)

Further analysis sent forward by Betsy Smith, who began her letter by pointing out that they felt the first strike "close to 10:30 a.m." She goes on to say, "I believe strongly that there is a great deal to be learned from this incident. First and foremost that if we waited for rescue near the top of the Grand, we would have risked being benighted. We would have also had to sit out the storm that came later in the afternoon. If we were benighted, [I] would have lost [my] left arm from the elbow down and [my] right hand, according to the doctor. Walker would have chanced losing his foot. Kline would have been risking his life, considering the air in his chest should have collapsed a lung. It was due to Kline's experience that he was able to build enough improvised anchors (with the gear that wasn't melted) to lower himself, Walker, and Smith to the upper saddle."

(Editor's Note: This was the Jenny Lake Rangers' largest rescue ever. Over the course of nine hours, seven people were flown from 13,200 feet and nine others were flown out from other locations. In all, 92 emergency workers became involved. The long narrative above should help the reader understand some of the decisions, intricacies, technical difficulties, and dedication required for such an operation.)

SLIP ON ROCK – BOULDER FIELD
Wyoming, Grand Teton National Park, Garnet Canyon Boulder Field

On July 22, in the early afternoon, I received a call from Exum Mountain Guide Trevor Deighton. He said that a member of his party had sustained an isolated right lower leg injury while descending through the Boulder Field in Garnet Canyon. The patient, Scott Hanson (43), had slipped on a rock, trapping his lower leg and causing the injury. Mr. Deighton caught Mr. Hanson before further injury occurred. Mr. Deighton told me that the accident happened at 1400 and that he had had to hike down canyon over a mile to get cell phone reception to make the report. I told Mr. Deighton to return to the site and that Rangers would be flown to the Meadows in Garnet Canyon to assist.

A briefing and risk assessment were conducted at the Rescue Cache. Rangers Vidak and Schuster were flown to a landing zone in Garnet Canyon and hiked down canyon to the patient by 1530. Ranger Schuster determined that Hanson had an isolated right lower leg injury with a possible fracture. Given the late hour of the day, rescuer fatigue associated with the unrelated, yet ongoing rescue and additional patient stress that would result from an extended evacuation by ground, the decision was made to extract the patient via helicopter short-haul.

Analysis

The Boulder Field in Garnet Canyon requires focus as one moves amongst and around the boulders. Use of hands is required as one lowers from or climbs over the boulders. Some of the granite blocks can be slick.. Whether due to inattention, fatigue, loose rock, and/or a slick foothold, Mr. Hanson unfortunately lost his footing at an inopportune time. (Source: Scott Guenther, Incident Commander)

VARIOUS STRANDED CLIMBERS
Wyoming, Devils Tower National Monument, Devils Tower

On October 30th, rangers received a phone call from Crook County dispatch regarding a group of climbers who were stuck on the south side of Devils Tower with a rope caught in a crack. They had no headlamps or proper cold weather clothing and had only a little food and water with them.

The five climbers, all from Iowa, were on a single-day climb to the summit via the Durrance Route when the incident occurred. Two of them reached the summit around 4:00 p.m. The climbers then descended to The Meadows, a relatively flat section on the south side of Devils Tower about 120 feet from the summit. One of them rappelled to a point about 140 feet below The Meadows.

The plan was for the remaining four to pull the rope back up, for three of them to be lowered, and for the fifth and final person to rappel down and join them. The rope, however, got stuck. The first climber then called for assistance.

Rangers Drew Gilmour, Tim Raaf and Joe Stiver responded and enlisted three local climbers—Keith Noback, Dave Schrall, and Chris Engle—in the rescue operation. Noback and Schrall started climbing the Durrance Route at 10 p.m., reaching the stranded climbers at 4:00 a.m. Noback, a local doctor, completed a brief medical assessment of the climbers, with particular attention to the possibility of hypothermia.

All five climbers were cold and tired, but able to complete the rappel down. Engle, waiting at the bottom of the Durrance Route, sent the climbers down the last 120 foot rappel to awaiting rangers and local fire and EMS personnel. All climbers returned safely, with only minor signs of hypothermia.

The temperature at 3:30 a.m. was 33 degrees, with light snow falling and winds blowing from 25 to 30 mph and gusting to 45 mph. (Source: Tim Raaf, Seasonal Ranger)

(Editor's Note: In April, two stranded climbers (in their 20s) were aided by rangers as a result of their rappel rope getting jammed in a crack. In July, four stranded climbers (again, all in 20s) were also rescued. Two of them were stuck near the top and the other two, friends who had ascended to help them, became stranded as well. The geology of DTNM often results in ropes jamming in the cracks. It used to be boots as well, back in the days when boots were worn.)

STATISTICAL TABLES

TABLE I
REPORTED MOUNTAINEERING ACCIDENTS

	Number of Accidents Reported		Total Persons Involved		Injured		Fatalities	
	USA	CAN	USA	CAN	USA	CAN	USA	CAN
1951	15		22		11		3	
1952	31		35		17		13	
1953	24		27		12		12	
1954	31		41		31		8	
1955	34		39		28		6	
1956	46		72		54		13	
1957	45		53		28		18	
1958	32		39		23		11	
1959	42	2	56	2	31	0	19	2
1960	47	4	64	12	37	8	19	4
1961	49	9	61	14	45	10	14	4
1962	71	1	90	1	64	0	19	1
1963	68	11	79	12	47	10	19	2
1964	53	11	65	16	44	10	14	3
1965	72	0	90	0	59	0	21	0
1966	67	7	80	9	52	6	16	3
1967	74	10	110	14	63	7	33	5
1968	70	13	87	19	43	12	27	5
1969	94	11	125	17	66	9	29	2
1970	129	11	174	11	88	5	15	5
1971	110	17	138	29	76	11	31	7
1972	141	29	184	42	98	17	49	13
1973	108	6	131	6	85	4	36	2
1974	96	7	177	50	75	1	26	5
1975	78	7	158	22	66	8	19	2
1976	137	16	303	31	210	9	53	6
1977	121	30	277	49	106	21	32	11
1978	118	17	221	19	85	6	42	10
1979	100	36	137	54	83	17	40	19
1980	191	29	295	85	124	26	33	8
1981	97	43	223	119	80	39	39	6
1982	140	48	305	126	120	43	24	14
1983	187	29	442	76	169	26	37	7
1984	182	26	459	63	174	15	26	6
1985	195	27	403	62	190	22	17	3
1986	203	31	406	80	182	25	37	14

	Number of Accidents Reported		Total Persons Involved		Injured		Fatalities	
	USA	CAN	USA	CAN	USA	CAN	USA	CAN
1987	192	25	377	79	140	23	32	9
1988	156	18	288	44	155	18	24	4
1989	141	18	272	36	124	11	17	9
1990	136	25	245	50	125	24	24	4
1991	169	20	302	66	147	11	18	6
1992	175	17	351	45	144	11	43	6
1993	132	27	274	50	121	17	21	1
1994	158	25	335	58	131	25	27	5
1995	168	24	353	50	134	18	37	7
1996	139	28	261	59	100	16	31	6
1997	158	35	323	87	148	24	31	13
1998	138	24	281	55	138	18	20	1
1999	123	29	248	69	91	20	17	10
2000	150	23	301	36	121	23	24	7
2001	150	22	276	47	138	14	16	2
2002	139	27	295	29	105	23	34	6
2003	118	29	231	32	105	22	18	6
2004	160	35	311	30	140	16	35	14
2005	111	19	176	41	85	14	34	7
2006	109		227		89		21	
2007	113		211		95		15	
2008	112		203		96		19	
2009	126		240		112		23	
2010	185		389		151		34	
Totals	6,756	958	12,438	2003	5,701	715	1,485	292

TABLE II

Geographical Districts	1951–2009			2010		
	Number of Accidents	Deaths	Total Persons Involved	Number of Accidents	Deaths	Total Persons Involved
CANADA*						
Alberta	520	142	1033			
British Columbia	317	119	641			
Yukon Territory	37	28	77			
New Brunswick	1	0	0			
Ontario	37	9	67			
Quebec	31	10	63			
East Arctic	8	2	21			
West Arctic	2	2	2			
Practice Cliffs[1]	20	2	36			
UNITED STATES						
Alaska	542	197	919	13	4	27
Arizona, Nevada Texas	97	18	177	3	0	8
Atlantic–North	1026	150	1763	21	1	38
Atlantic–South	123	28	217	20	5	40
California	1331	298	637	53	4	87
Central	136	18	219	0	0	0
Colorado	800	219	2378	41	10	87
Montana, Idaho South Dakota	86	35	140	4	0	8
Oregon	218	116	486	3	1	6
Utah, New Mexico	181	60	332	3	0	5
Washington	1062	324	925	12	4	47
Wyoming	576	135	1043	12	5	36

*No data from 2006–2010

[1]This category includes bouldering, artificial climbing walls, buildings, and so forth. These are also added to the count of each province, but not to the total count, though that error has been made in previous years. The Practice Cliffs category has been removed from the U.S. data.

TABLE III

	1951–09 USA	1959–04 CAN.	2010 USA	2010 CAN.
Terrain				
Rock	4607	528	128	
Snow	2408	355	53	
Ice	278	15	4	
River	15	3	0	
Unknown	22	10	0	
Ascent or Descent				
Ascent	3668	587	122	
Descent	1068	371	55	
Unknown	251	13	5	
Other[N.B.]	9	0	3	
Immediate Cause				
Fall or slip on rock	3648	290	97	
Slip on snow or ice	1050	207	21	
Falling rock, ice, or object	636	137	17	
Exceeding abilities	555	32	2	
Illness[1]	409	26	11	
Stranded	351	53	17	
Avalanche	299	127	5	
Rappel Failure/Error[2]	303	47	12	
Exposure	278	14	0	
Loss of control/glissade	215	17	0	
Nut/chock pulled out	243	9	11	
Failure to follow route	213	30	6	
Fall into crevasse/moat	167	50	2	
Faulty use of crampons	115	6	0	
Piton/ice screw pulled out	95	13	0	
Ascending too fast	67	0	5	
Skiing[3]	58	11	6	
Lightning	46	7	1	
Equipment failure	16	3	0	
Other[4]	522	37	27	
Unknown	61	10	0	
Contributory Causes				
Climbing unroped	1021	165	10	
Exceeding abilities	917	202	38	
Placed no/inadequate protection	794	96	19	
Inadequate equipment/clothing	701	70	16	
Weather	481	67	14	
Climbing alone	408	69	12	

	1951–09 USA	1959–04 CAN	2010 USA	2010 CAN
No hard hat	354	71	5	
Inadequate belay[2]	228	28	14	
Nut/chock pulled out	201	32	8	
Poor position	188	20	16	
Darkness	150	21	15	
Party separated	117	12	1	
Failure to test holds	105	32	0	
Piton/ice screw pulled out	86	13	0	
Failed to follow directions	73	12	0	
Exposure	64	16	1	
Illness[1]	40	9	0	
Equipment failure	11	7	0	
Other[4]	271	100	10	
Age of Individuals				
Under 15	1246	12	0	
15–20	1288	203	6	
21–25	1439	257	35	
26–30	1327	211	41	
31–35	2006	114	26	
36–50	1307	143	43	
Over 50	284	31	31	
Unknown	2029	530	57	
Experience Level				
None/Little	1785	304	41	
Moderate (1 to 3 years)	1650	354	27	
Experienced	2099	440	81	
Unknown	2138	559	99	
Month of Year				
January	241	25	1	
February	213	55	9	
March	321	68	6	
April	421	39	8	
May	957	62	23	
June	1100	70	40	
July	1174	254	24	
August	1075	184	27	
September	1191	75	24	
October	474	42	11	
November	203	20	6	
December	105	24	6	
Unknown	17	1	1	

	1951–09 USA	1959–04 CAN	2010 USA	2010 CAN
Type of Injury/Illness (Data since 1984)				
Fracture	1352	223	57	
Laceration	737	71	19	
Abrasion	361	76	17	
Bruise	512	83	25	
Sprain/strain	385	33	29	
Concussion	266	28	8	
Hypothermia	162	16	7	
Frostbite	134	12	2	
Dislocation	137	16	9	
Puncture	52	13	1	
Acute Mountain Sickness	45	0	1	
HAPE	74	0	7	
HACE	25	0	3	
Other[5]	350	49	7	
None	265	188	30	

N.B. Some accidents happen when climbers are at the top or bottom of a route, not climbing. They may be setting up a belay or rappel or are just not anchored when they fall. (This category created in 2001. The category "unknown" is primarily because of solo climbers.)

[1] These illnesses/injuries, which led directly or indirectly to the accident, included: kidney stones; pre-existing atrial irregularity; HAPE (4).

[2] These included: clipping in to gear loop; rope too short; no knot in end of rope (4); distraction (4); lowered off end of rope; belayer pulled partner off; inadequate back-up; threaded lowering rope through nylon sling which burned through; slack in belay rope; carabiner not closed.

[3] This category was set up originally for ski mountaineering. Backcountry touring or snowshoeing incidents—even if one gets avalanched—are not in the data.

[4] These included: distraction (4); communication problems (3); unable to self-arrest (3); leader broke ice dam, releasing water and ice that hit partner; failure to pay attention to weather patterns; dislodging rock caused fall; cornice gave away; ice column collapsed; "summit fever;" inadequate self-rescue skills; tangled in climbing rope—caused fall; misjudged pendulum swing distance; climber unclipped from team and disappeared.

[5] These included: dehydration; exhaustion; thumb amputation; hyperextension; back spasms; internal injuries; chest trauma; 1,000 bee stings; dehydration; rope burn.

(Editor's Note: Under the category "other," many of the particular items will have been recorded under a general category. For example, the climber who dislodges a rock that falls on another climber would be coded as "Falling Rock/Object." A climber who has a hand or foot-hold come loose and falls would be coded as "Fall On Rock" and "Other" — and most often includes "Failure To Test Holds;" rappel and belay errors are also recorded as "Fall on Rock," and so forth.)

MOUNTAIN RESCUE UNITS IN NORTH AMERICA

**Denotes team fully certified—Technical Rock,
Snow & Ice, Wilderness Search;
S, R, SI = certified partially in Search, Rock, and/or Snow & Ice

ALASKA

Alaska Mountain Rescue Group. PO Box 241102, Anchorage,
AK 99524. www.amrg.org

Denali National Park SAR. PO Box 588, Talkeetna, AK 99676.
Dena_talkeetna@nps.gov

Juneau Mountain Rescue, Inc. 2970 Foster Ave., Juneau, AK 99801

Sitka Mountain Search and Rescue. 209 Lake St., Sitka, AK 99835

US Army Alaskan Warfare Training Center. #2900 501 Second St., APO AP 96508

ARIZONA

Apache Rescue Team. PO Box 100, St. Johns, AZ 85936

Arizona Department Of Public Safety Air Rescue. Phoenix, Flagstaff, Tucson,
Kingman, AZ

Arizona Division Of Emergency Services. Phoenix, AZ

Grand Canyon National Park Rescue Team. PO Box 129, Grand Canyon, AZ 86023

**Central Arizona Mountain Rescue Team/Maricopa County Sheriff's Office
MR.** PO Box 4004 Phoenix, AZ 85030. www.mcsomr.org

Sedona Fire District Special Operations Rescue Team. 2860 Southwest Dr.,
Sedona, AZ 86336. ropes@sedona.net

Southern Arizona Rescue Assn/Pima County Sheriff's Office. PO Box 12892,
Tucson, AZ 85732. http://hambox.theriver.com/sarci/sara01.html

CALIFORNIA

Altadena Mountain Rescue Team. 780 E. Altadena Dr., Altadena, CA 91001
www.altadenasheriffs.org/rescue/amrt.html

Bay Area Mountain Rescue Team. PO Box 19184, Stanford, CA 94309 bamru@
hooked.net

California Office of Emergency Services. 2800 Meadowview Rd., Sacramento, CA.
95832. warning.center@oes.ca.gov

China Lake Mountain Rescue Group. PO Box 2037, Ridgecrest, CA 93556
www.clmrg.org

Inyo County Sheriff's Posse SAR. PO Box 982, Bishop, CA 93514
inyocosar@juno.com

Joshua Tree National Park SAR. 74485 National Monument Drive,
Twenty Nine Palms, CA 92277. patrick_suddath@nps.gov

Malibu Mountain Rescue Team. PO Box 222, Malibu, CA 90265.
www.mmrt.org

Montrose SAR Team. PO Box 404, Montrose, CA 91021

Riverside Mountain Rescue Unit. PO Box 5444, Riverside,
CA 92517. www.rmru.org rmru@bigfoot.com

San Bernardino County Sheriff's Cave Rescue Team. 655 E. Third St.
San Bernardino, CA 92415
www.sbsd-vfu.org/units/SAR/SAR203/sar203_1.htm

San Bernardino County So/West Valley SAR. 13843 Peyton Dr., Chino Hills, CA
91709.

San Diego Mountain Rescue Team. PO Box 81602, San Diego, CA 92138. www.sdmrt.org

San Dimas Mountain Rescue Team. PO Box 35, San Dimas, CA 91773

Santa Barbara SAR Team. PO Box 6602, Santa Barbara, CA 93160-6602

Santa Clarita Valley SAR/L.A.S.O. 23740 Magic Mountain Parkway, Valencia, CA 91355. http://members.tripod.com/scvrescue/

Sequoia-Kings Canyon National Park Rescue Team. Three Rivers, CA 93271

Sierra Madre SAR. PO Box 24, Sierra Madre, CA 91025. www.mra.org/smsrt.html

Tuolumne County Search and Rescue Sheriff's Office. 28 North Lower Sunset Drive, Sonora, CA 95370.

Ventura County SAR. 2101 E. Olson Rd, Thousand Oaks, CA 91362 www.vcsar.org

Yosemite National Park Rescue Team. PO Box 577-SAR, Yosemite National Park, CA 95389

COLORADO

Alpine Rescue Team. PO Box 934, Evergreen, CO 80437 www.alpinerescueteam.org

Colorado Ground SAR. 2391 Ash St, Denver, CO 80222 www.coloradowingcap.org/CGSART/Default.htm

Crested Butte SAR. PO Box 485, Crested Butte, CO 81224

Douglas County Search And Rescue. PO Box 1102, Castle Rock, CO 80104. www.dcsarco.org info@dcsarco.org

El Paso County SAR. 3950 Interpark Dr, Colorado Springs, CO 80907-9028. www.epcsar.org

Eldorado Canyon State Park. PO Box B, Eldorado Springs, CO 80025

Grand County SAR. Box 172, Winter Park, CO 80482

Larimer County SAR. 1303 N. Shields St., Fort Collins, CO 80524. www.fortnet. org/LCSAR/ lcsar@co.larimer.co.us

Mountain Rescue Aspen. 630 W. Main St, Aspen, CO 81611 www.mountainrescueaspen.org

Park County SAR, CO. PO Box 721, Fairplay, CO 80440

Rocky Mountain National Park Rescue Team. Estes Park, CO 80517

Rocky Mountain Rescue Group. PO Box Y, Boulder, CO 80306 www.colorado.edu/StudentGroups/rmrg/ rmrg@colorado.edu

Routt County SAR. PO Box 772837, Steamboat Springs, CO 80477 RCSAR@co.routt.co.us

Summit County Rescue Group. PO Box 1794, Breckenridge, CO 80424

Vail Mountain Rescue Group. PO Box 1597, Vail, CO 81658 http://sites.netscape.net/vailmra/homepage vmrg@vail.net

Western State College Mountain Rescue Team. Western State College Union, Gunnison, CO 81231. org_mrt@western.edu

IDAHO

Bonneville County SAR. 605 N. Capital Ave, Idaho Falls, ID 83402 www.srv.net/~jrcase/bcsar.html

Idaho Mountain SAR. PO Box 741, Boise, ID 83701.www.imsaru.org rsksearch@aol.com

MAINE
Acadia National Park SAR. Bar Harbor, Maine

MARYLAND
**Maryland Sar Group. 5434 Vantage Point Road, Columbia, MD 21044
Peter_McCabe@Ed.gov

MONTANA
Glacier National Park SAR. PO Box 128, Glacier National Park,
West Glacier, MT 59936
Flathead County Search and Rescue. 920 South Main St., Kalispell, MT 59901.
Sheriff's Office phone: 406-758-5585.

NEVADA
**Las Vegas Metro PD SAR. 4810 Las Vegas Blvd., South Las Vegas,
NV 89119. www.lvmpdsar.com

NEW MEXICO
**Albuquerque Mountain Rescue Council. PO Box 53396, Albuquerque,
NM 87153. www.abq.com/amrc/ albrescu@swcp.com

NEW HAMPSHIRE
Appalachian Mountain Club. Pinkham Notch Camp, Gorham, NH 03581
Mountain Rescue Service. PO Box 494, North Conway, NH 03860

NEW YORK
76 SAR. 243 Old Quarry Rd., Feura Bush, NY 12067
Mohonk Preserve Rangers. PO Box 715, New Paltz, NY 12561
NY State Forest Rangers. 50 Wolf Rd., Room 440C, Albany, NY 12233

OREGON
**Corvallis Mountain Rescue Unit. PO Box 116, Corvallis, OR 97339
www.cmrv.peak.org
(S, R) Deschutes County SAR. 63333 West Highway 20, Bend, OR 97701
**Eugene Mountain Rescue. PO Box 20, Eugene, OR 97440
**Hood River Crag Rats Rescue Team. 2880 Thomsen Rd., Hood River,
OR 97031
**Portland Mountain Rescue. PO Box 5391, Portland, OR 97228
www.pmru.org info@pmru.org

PENNSYLVANNIA
**Allegheny Mountain Rescue Group. c/o Mercy Hospital,
1400 Locust, Pittsburgh, PA 15219. www.asrc.net/amrg
**Wilderness Emergency Strike Team. 11 North Duke Street, Lancaster,
PA 17602. www.west610.org

UTAH
**Davis County Sheriff's SAR. PO Box 800, Farmington, UT 84025. www.dcsar.org
Rocky Mountain Rescue Dogs. 3353 S. Main #122, Salt Lake City, UT 84115

Salt Lake County Sheriff's SAR. 3510 South 700 West, Salt Lake City, UT 84119

San Juan County Emergency Services. PO Box 9, Monticello, UT 84539

Utah County Sherrif's SAR. PO Box 330, Provo, UT 84603.
ucsar@utah.uswest.net

Weber County Sheriff's Mountain Rescue. 745 Nancy Dr, Ogden,
UT 84403. http://planet.weber.edu/mru

Zion National Park SAR. Springdale, UT 84767

VERMONT
Stowe Mountain Rescue. P.O. Box 291, Stowe, VT 05672. www.stowevt.org/htt/

VIRGINIA
Air Force Rescue Coordination Center. Suite 101, 205 Dodd Building,
Langley AFB, VA 23665. www2.acc.af.mil/afrcc/airforce.rescue@usa.net

WASHINGTON STATE
Bellingham Mountain Rescue Council. PO Box 292, Bellingham, WA 98225

Central Washington Mountain Rescue Council. PO Box 2663, Yakima, WA
98907. www.nwinfo.net/~cwmr/ cwmr@nwinfo.net

Everett Mountain Rescue Unit, Inc. 5506 Old Machias Road, Snohomish, WA
98290-5574. emrui@aol.com

Mount Rainier National Park Rescue Team. Longmire, WA 98397

North Cascades National Park Rescue Team. 728 Ranger Station Rd,
Marblemount, WA 98267

Olympic Mountain Rescue. PO Box 4244, Bremerton, WA 98312
www.olympicmountainrescue.org information@olympicmountainrescue.org

Olympic National Park Rescue Team. 600 Park Ave, Port Angeles, WA 98362

Seattle Mountain Rescue. PO Box 67, Seattle, WA 98111
www.eskimo.com/~pc22/SMR/smr.html

Skagit Mountain Rescue. PO Box 2, Mt. Vernon, WA 98273

Tacoma Mountain Rescue. PO Box 696, Tacoma, WA 98401
www.tmru.org

North Country Volcano Rescue Team. 404 S. Parcel Ave, Yacolt, WA 98675
www.northcountryems.org/vrt/index.html

WASHINGTON, DC
National Park Service, EMS/SAR Division. Washington, DC

US Park Police Aviation. Washington, DC

WYOMING
Grand Teton National Park Rescue Team. PO Box 67, Moose, WY 83012

Park County SAR, WY. Park County SO, 1131 11th, Cody, WY 82412

CANADA
North Shore Rescue Team. 147 E. 14th St, North Vancouver, B.C.,
Canada V7L 2N4

Rocky Mountain House SAR. Box 1888, Rocky Mountain House, Alberta,
Canada T0M 1T0

MOUNTAIN RESCUE ASSOCIATION
PO Box 880868
San Diego, CA 92168-0868
www.mra.org

Neil Van Dyke, President
Stowe Mountain Rescue, VT
P.O. Box 291, Stowe, VT 05672
vp@mra.org
802-253-9060
Term Expires June 2010

Doug Wessen, Vice President
Juneau Mountain Rescue, Inc., AK
2970 Foster Ave., Juneau, AK 99801
dougwessen@gmail.com
907-586-4834
Term Expires 2010

John Chang, Secretary/Treasurer
Bay Area Mountain Rescue
PO Box 19184, Stanford, CA 94309
sectreas@mra.org
925-699-2506 (cell)
Term Expires 2011

Jim Frank, Member-at-Large
Santa Barbara SAR Team
P.O. Box 6602, Santa Barbara, CA 93160
j.frank@impulse.net
805-961-1621 (w)   805-452-3261 (cell)
Term Expires 2011

David Clarke, Member-at –Large
42271 S. Coleman Rd., Sandy, OR, 97055
daveclarke@frontier.com
503-784-6341

Kayley Bell, Executive Secretary
PO Box 880868, San Diego, CA 92168
info@mra.org
858-229-4295 (h)   951-317-5635 (cell)